REFLEC

fo

BUSY
PEOPLE

Making Time for
Ourselves, Jesus, and God

GERALD O'COLLINS, SJ

Paulist Press
New York/Mahwah, NJ

The Scripture quotations contained herein are from the author's own translation. Used by permission.

Cover design by Joy Taylor
Book design by Lynn Else

Copyright © 2009 by Gerald O'Collins, SJ

Cover photo copyright © by Gill Henshall

Library of Congress Cataloging-in-Publication Data

O'Collins, Gerald.
    Reflections for busy people : making time for ourselves, Jesus, and God / Gerald O'Collins.
        p. cm.
    Includes index.
    ISBN 978-0-8091-4606-2 (alk. paper)
    1. Meditations. I. Title.
    BV4832.3.O26 2009
    242—dc22

                                                                2009011645

Published by Paulist Press
997 Macarthur Boulevard
Mahwah, New Jersey 07430

www.paulistpress.com

Printed and bound in Canada

Contents

CONTENTS

Preface

This book is designed for people who are busy but still want to take time out to face the deeper realities of life. They feel the need to be in touch with themselves, with Jesus, and with God.

Every now and then, personal questions arise to challenge us: Who are we? What are we doing? What does, and what should, life mean to us? These are urgent and important questions. Yet we will not understand our real selves unless we allow further questions to arise: Who is Jesus? What has he done and what is he doing for us? What should he mean to us? Who is God? What is God doing for us? What should God mean to us?

My hope and prayer for you, dear readers, is that pondering the short chapters of this book will let your hidden selves come to you, even as Jesus comes to you and God comes to you. Through encountering yourselves, Jesus, and God even fleetingly, you will be enabled to see the real state of things and accept an authentic agenda for your lives.

This book offers vignettes or short essays on what it is to be human, on what Jesus is and does as our Savior, and what God is and does for us as our home here and hereafter. We move from the human condition to Jesus, our Savior and, finally, to God, our home. Inevitably and rightly, the three parts will intermesh. Let us begin with five themes that touch deeply our human condition: our desires, our prayer, the faces of others, our common fate in death, and sin (both sins of commission and those of omission).

REFLECTIONS FOR BUSY PEOPLE

I am grateful to the many audiences to whom I have presented some of what follows. They have encouraged me to think it worthwhile to set down for a wider readership what they heard. I also wish to thank Alan and Verity Mitchell for the permission to use "The Easter Diary," which they wrote about their son Christopher who died at six months of age.

This book is dedicated to the Jesuit friends with whom I have shared life at John Sinnott House in Wimbledon, London.

St. Mary's University College,
Twickenham, England
April 8, 2008

Part One

Ourselves

1

The Hungers of the Heart

What is it to be truly human? What is it that's worth setting our hearts on? At least every now and then, we feel that there is more to life than a frenetic round of producing and consuming. Why should we let other people and faceless forces run our lives? Sooner or later, we are visited by a yearning to break free and stop allowing others to set the agenda for us. At some point in our story, all of us dream of thinking things through and repossessing ourselves.

Within each of us, many desires clamor to be heard. Which desires deserve to be examined, treasured, and followed? Recommending such self-scrutiny does not aim at encouraging anyone to become self-absorbed and put all one's personal energies into securing "my" personal achievement and spiritual renewal. Rather, it is an invitation to dive deeper and reflect upon the innate desires that shape our human condition and fuel its restless drive for new directions in our lives.

For many years, the summer break from teaching has seen me traveling around the world and lecturing in summer programs for various colleges, seminaries, and universities. Whenever I am free on Sundays, I am happy to celebrate the Eucharist in some local parish. Facing such audiences for the first time calls for some quick way of establishing contact with all the people attending the service. I have often begun by saying, "My name is Father Gerry O'Collins, and this is my first time in your parish. I have never met any of you before, but I know one thing about every person sharing in the Eucharist this morning: Each one of you is incessantly searching for the fullness of life, meaning, and love. That fullness is to be found only in God."

However well or badly my tactic for focusing attention works, it touches the deepest drives of our human existence: what we constantly seek to avoid and what we constantly long to experience. In innumerable forms, we repeatedly face death, situations that seem meaningless or even absurd, isolation, or even hatred. But hope lifts us beyond such crippling circumstances and makes us imagine that things could be very different. We yearn for life, meaning, and love. A dynamic search to receive life, to find meaning, and to love and be loved shapes our common human condition.

Faced with dramatic or less-dramatic situations, human beings may feel threatened by death in its various shapes and forms. They may be overwhelmed by a sense of injustice and meaningless absurdity. They may be abandoned, cruelly treated, and simply hated. But then they may be given life; they may experience a deeper meaning and order in things; and they may know themselves to be the object of loving goodness. Such experiences can make people long even more for a gift of life, meaning, and love that will change everything.

These experiences and longings point, I believe, to the God who is the Fullness of Life, Total Meaning, and Infinite Love. Part Three of this book will take up this way of thinking about the Trinity. Here, let me simply say that this view of the Trinity is compelling in a world that in some ways seems to be becoming more deadly, more absurd, and more cruel.

Unquestionably, we can describe the hungers of our human heart in various ways. Yet ultimately, it seems to me, they assume a triple shape: a primordial desire for life, meaning, and love.

First, we hunger and thirst to live. People may argue about where to find life. But all yearn for life in its full abundance (John 10:10) and pray not to be sucked under by the fearful forces of annihilation.

Second, we want things to make sense. When goals are clear and meaning comes through brightly, we can cope with great, even immense, difficulties. Absurd situations leave us floating aimlessly and without a compass. In the words of the British philosopher and historian Michael Oakshott, "to be human is to live in a world of meaning; to be without meaning is to be a stranger to the human condition."

Third, we have a deep need to be loved by others and to love others. Love *does* make our world go round. We yearn to be recognized and encouraged by those who love us. Where love is concerned, our hearts are a "bottomless gorge," as the poet and artist William Blake put it. Or, to vary the image, our hearts soak up the love they receive like a sponge that is never saturated.

We crave for a life that is absolutely full and will never end. We search for a meaning that will light up everything. We hunger for a perfect love that will be utterly satisfying. God is the fulfillment of this primordial yearning. God is the One who will completely and finally satisfy all our hunger and quench our thirst.

I have suggested a triple search, but we might reduce it all to one basic yearning. We all want to be loved. Deep within each of us, there is a tremendous hunger to be cherished and to feel that someone loves us completely, unconditionally, and without limit. No human being can give us this kind of love and satisfy our hungry hearts. Ultimately it is only being loved by God and loving God that will truly satisfy us. To echo the words with which St. Augustine of Hippo began his *Confessions*, our hearts are made for God and will not rest until they rest in God.

It is in prayer that this primordial yearning expresses itself and finds its true compass. Let us turn to what prayer involves in the next few chapters.

―――――――――――――――

2

Letting Ourselves Be Loved

There is a story about a man who was very anxious over the state of the world and went off to talk about his worries with an old holy woman. She lived alone as a hermit and spent most of the day in prayer. When the man arrived at the hermitage, he started talking about all the evil and suffering that afflict the whole world. He concluded his speech by saying: "All these problems would be solved if we loved each other more." "No," said the hermit. "What really matters is God's love. The problems would be solved if we let *God* love us more."

Letting God love us more could well be a description of prayer. Spending regular time in prayer with God means just that: letting God love us into life and then into more life, and so growing as human beings.

Many years ago, I spent a week praying in a retreat center out in the countryside in Southern California. The house itself was pleasant but fairly ordinary. Its surroundings, however, were quite extraordinary. The house stood right in the middle of a vast nursery for shrubs and young trees. Around us, row after row of small pines, cypresses, fruit trees, and other kinds of trees and shrubs ran off into the distance. There seemed to be thousands of rows out there. The owner claimed that he had one million trees and shrubs on his property.

Early every morning, workers moved along the rows watering the trees and plants. Every day the sun came up in a cloudless sky, and the temperature rose to about ninety degrees. With all that constant watering and the daily sun, you could almost see the trees and shrubs growing right before your eyes.

Prayer is something like that. It means standing before God and letting God's love feed us, warm us, and make us grow. We need the sun and water of divine love to make us survive and flourish. If we stand regularly before God in prayer, divine love will come flooding over us to nourish and transform our lives. When we let ourselves be loved by God, we will become much more beautiful than any of those trees or shrubs growing up straight in the sunshine.

The hundreds of thousands of plants and trees in that California nursery had no choice. They were watered each day and flooded with sunshine. They grew automatically. We have to choose to take our place in the nursery of God's love. If we do so, we will find that love shining down on us. Through receiving in prayer the warmth of God's love, we will grow humanly, spiritually, and *wonderfully*.

St. Theophan the Recluse—a Russian monk, bishop, and then hermit (d. 1894)—knew what prayer brings: "Prayer is the test of everything; prayer is also the source of everything....If prayer is right, everything is right. For prayer will not allow anything to go wrong."

Through prayer, God lets nothing go wrong. Prayer brings us life and light—a fact expressed by an African proverb: "Where there is love, it is never dark." Nothing can be more important each day than enjoying, through prayer, God's love and light.

If we let God's love beam down on us day by day, the world *will* be a better place. That daily prayer will make our lives grow up to heaven more directly and beautifully than any pine or cypress in California.

From being near him in Rome for over twenty-five years, I saw how prayer happened in the life of someone deeply concerned with the sufferings and problems of the whole world: Pope John Paul II. Let me turn to his example of prayer.

3

The Busy Pope with Time to Pray

"Her life was committed totally to the poor and wrapped in prayer." That was how Pope John Paul II summed up the life of Mother Teresa of Calcutta. Listening to these words during her October 2003 beatification, I thought to myself, "The pope could be talking about himself."

It is hard to imagine a busier life than the one that John Paul II led during more than the twenty-six years of his pontificate. He completed 104 pastoral visits outside Italy and 146 within Italy. As bishop of Rome, he visited 317 of its 333 parishes. No other pope ever encountered as many individuals as John Paul II did.

Nearly eighteen million people attended the general audiences he regularly held on Wednesdays. One can rattle off almost endless statistics to show what an incredibly busy life he led. Like Mother Teresa, he was totally committed to the poor and to everyone else. Time flew by for him but Pope John Paul II always made time for prayer.

Occasionally he prayed in places that powerfully lend themselves to prayer. On a visit to the Holy Land in 2000, he went down the steps on his old, aching legs to pray in the cave of the nativity, the grotto where ancient tradition locates the birth of Jesus. Often John Paul II also prayed in everyday places, like his private chapel in Vatican City.

He knew very well the famous statement from St. Augustine: "God is closer to me than I am to myself." In and through prayer, the pope constantly let himself experience the divine presence. Like Augustine, he prayed: "Lord, that I might know myself, that I might know Thee!"

Those who lived with the pope in the small papal household saw just how many hours he spent in prayer. Millions of Catholics and other Christians around the world witnessed the deep devotion with which he celebrated Mass or led them in other forms of worship. Only someone whose whole life was bathed in personal prayer could lead others with such a reverent sense of God's nearness.

A public fruit of John Paul II's life of prayer came in his encyclical letters and other documents. He liked to end them with heartfelt petitions expressing in prayer the heart of the particular teaching he had just developed. These profound prayers could come only from someone who constantly gave hours of time to the presence of the Lord.

We can often feel how little time we have for praying with others, for reading scriptures, and for spending even a few minutes of our day alone with God. The things that fill up our day demand so much of our attention.

We can even be tempted to excuse ourselves and think that we are in regular touch with God simply by being involved with people. By giving our time, our attention, and our energies to others, we think, aren't we surely reaching God?

Yet all of us have experienced at least occasionally the quiet peace and real strength that can flood into us from time spent in prayer. We know, too, how mere activity, even activity in the service of others, can leave us empty and unsatisfied. We need constant prayer to connect us with the source of all spiritual strength, the unseen God.

If reflection on our own experience is not enough to motivate us into prioritizing our time to pray, perhaps we can look at the life of John Paul II and Mother Teresa. Shining examples of people utterly committed to others, they drew from hours of prayer the strength to carry forward their tenacious work for a world in pain.

4

The Prayer of One Couple

Some years ago, I stayed a few days in New York with a friend. His wife Maureen had died some months earlier after a long battle with cancer.

Photographs of Maureen, her clothes, and other objects made her presence in that apartment still very real. But the thing that brought her back to me most vividly was her breviary, the book used by priests and many others for daily prayer. For years Maureen had joined her husband in the morning and the evening to pray together the Liturgy of the Hours.

The evening I arrived, my friend asked me to join him in prayer and handed me Maureen's breviary. Ribbons marked the pages where she could find the appropriate hymns, frequently used prayers like the Magnificat, and, of course, the psalms for the feasts and the different days of the weeks.

When I opened Maureen's breviary and began reciting vespers with her widowed husband, I felt as if I were entering into her prayer life and taking up the praise of God at the point when she had left off, died, and gone to enjoy the face-to-face vision of God in the utter happiness of heaven. It was a special privilege to be let into the daily Liturgy of the Hours that had fed the couple's spiritual life.

Why did they commit themselves faithfully for so many years to that daily program of prayer? They had come to see how beautiful and life-giving it was to join Jesus the high priest in singing, day by day, the praises of God. That, above all, is what we do in the Liturgy of the Hours: raise our minds and voices together in praising and thanking our ever-loving God.

Maureen and her husband had worked hard and enjoyed many material comforts. But they knew that, without their program of prayer together, they would weaken their clear vision of what their Christian life should mean as a married couple with children and grandchildren. They knew, too, the exquisite way such prayer unites our personal needs with the life and concerns of so many other believers everywhere.

The psalms provide the Liturgy of the Hours with a deeply personal feeling. Through the psalms, each of us can pour out our hearts to God. Through the psalms, we know God with our hearts rather than merely with our heads. By constantly praying the psalms, we experience God and grow in wonder at the divine gifts and in gratitude for the divine gifts. Without such wonder and gratitude, our life has no real depth.

Through praying together, Maureen and her husband enjoyed a profound and rich experience of the God they loved and trusted. But they also knew that they belonged to a worldwide chorus of praise, rising from all those men and women around the world who also recite and sing the Liturgy of the Hours.

Maureen's husband has fallen sick now, with the same cancer (melanoma) that took her away. He has found himself being treated in the same hospital and by some of the same medical personnel who cared for Maureen. His constant prayer with her has enabled him to understand how his life is now overshadowed by a condition that may soon unite him with her again when he passes from this world to the next. Love and prayer have brought them together here and hereafter.

Through life they shared in that universal chorus and prayer led by Christ in praise of our loving God. Why not join the choir and let Christ be your director in lifting up your hearts and minds in song and prayer?

5

Faces in Rome

Some people who spend time in Rome stamp their faces on the memory of the world. After being elected pope in October 1978, John Paul II lived in the eternal city until his death in April 2005. His travels to well over one hundred countries and, even more, the television networks brought his face to the world. However, of those who have spent part of their lives in Rome, his is not the only face that is instantly recognized by millions of people. Oscar Romero, the martyred archbishop of San Salvador, studied in Rome for five years (1937–42) and sometimes returned there on short visits. His face is known everywhere in Latin America and beyond.

For those of my generation, the faces of John Paul II and Oscar Romero gave rise to some demanding questions. Identifying them, we identified ourselves. But there have been other "Roman faces," never featured in the television news or on the front pages of the daily newspapers, who have shown me much about our common humanity. Teaching in Rome for thirty-three years (1973–2006) allowed me to meet some remarkable men and women. Their faces also conveyed answers to the questions: Who are we? And what are we doing? The faces of Luke, Lucia, Donatien, Anton, Bernadette, Innocent, and Patrick linger in my memory. I treasure what they revealed to me about the human condition and its wonderful possibilities.

Luke worked for thirty years as a prison chaplain in a country that enforced capital punishment. He attended hangings, standing on the gallows next to the condemned men and holding their hand before they were dropped with a rope around their necks. He remembered vividly the precise number of executions he witnessed—fifty-eight—as well as many details of what led up to each hanging. He knew how barbaric and useless the hangings were. But somehow, before the men died, he managed to reconcile to God every one of the condemned. I think it was the unaffected goodness and simplicity which shone from his rough-hewn face that touched all those hearts. No one has ever taught me more about human compassion.

Much more intellectual than Luke but patently good like him, Lucia came from a country which had fallen under military rule. The generals and their deputies were responsible for mass torture and murder. For years, the father of Lucia worked as a doctor in one of the military jails. That terrible period in her country's history had ended when I met Lucia; however, there was a constant edge of sadness on her face. Her life remained shadowed by the memory of a brutal violence that destroyed the lives of thousands of young people, and by her father's possible complicity in those crimes. Lucia left me with the haunting question: How would *I* keep working and surviving if I had learned a tragic truth about my own father? Her father had been trained to save lives, but for years had drawn his salary from an institution devoted to torture and killing.

By contrast, a constant serenity played across the face of Donatien. A great biblical scholar, he taught the Gospel of John and lived it. Until I listened to Donatien and read his writings, I had not fully appreciated two pervasive characteristics of this Gospel: the gripping stories of individuals who meet Jesus and are transformed through their encounter with him, and the evangelist's constant use of the verb *to believe*. John never uses the noun *belief*, or *faith* (*pistis*), but always the verb *believe* (*pisteuein*) or some equivalent. The verbal quality of this Gospel reflects the dynamic quality of faith. Not something to be boxed away, human faith exists actively in the aftermath of a life-transforming meeting with Jesus. The radiant joy that I witnessed on the face of Donatien mirrored beautifully the picture of the believing discipleship conveyed by John's Gospel.

A peaceful, cheerful person, Anton had spent the Second World War in two concentration camps. Arrested in November 1939, he was one of the first prisoners in what was to become Auschwitz. One of his prison duties was to clean the commander's office. He took the opportunity to switch on the radio and catch the BBC news. The German officer could be relied on to return exactly at the usual time, so listening to the radio was not unduly risky. What took courage was sharing the news with other prisoners. A single Judas could have sent Anton to his death. In the end, what probably saved his life was being transferred from Poland to Germany and the concentration camp in Dachau, where the killing of inmates was incidental, although widespread. Anton witnessed the rest of the war there. He emerged starving but remarkably intact as a human being and a Christian. In November, on the anniversary of the day on which he was first arrested, I would invite him to my room and drink his good health. He would also recall the day in May 1945 when he was set free by American forces under the command of General George Patton. "It took Patton to liberate me," Anton used to remark, with a smile on his face. I have never met anyone more unassuming and courageous.

After serving as a missionary in Africa, Bernadette came to Rome and spent years there as a senior councilor and then superior general of her religious institute. During that time she sometimes attended meetings of nuns and monks who belonged to Catholic and Orthodox monasteries and religious houses. Unlike dialogues between theologians of different churches, those meetings took place in a context of prayer and the sharing of spiritual experiences. A person of lively laughter, winning sweetness, and utter loyalty to her friends, Bernadette let slip every now and then the heart of her existence: a commitment to contemplative prayer that put her arms around the world. When she left Rome, she went to live as a hermit outside a village in the Cameroon Republic. The local people cherished her, but for years I expected to read a report one day that others had brutally murdered her. Fortunately, she came home to Europe, older and using a stick when she walks, but still refreshingly positive about a world and a Christianity in which there seem to be so many problems but so few solutions. In a tiny hermitage adorned with Eastern icons, her life is wrapped in prayer.

I do not know whether Bernadette ever met Innocent and Patrick, two Africans from Rwanda who spent five years studying in Rome, and who both took at least one course with me. We met each other at least once a week, as they lived in the college where I often went for the evening meal. Cheerfully sociable and modestly low-key, Patrick and Innocent went about life with straightforward dedication—a heroic dedication as I came to learn. They returned to Kigali and ran a center for reconciliation between Tutsis and Hutus. On the first day of the genocidal massacres in 1994, the militia came for them and hacked them to death. In their smiling, undramatic way, Patrick and Innocent taught me what modern martyrdom can involve.

The faces of these seven men and women stay with me as a lovely legacy from my Roman years. In very different ways, they answered my questions: Who are we? And what are we doing? They were all extraordinary people, even if none of them wanted to dramatize their lives. They all showed me what human beings can do if faith is at the heart of their existence.

6

Life Is Saturated with Death

In April 2005, nearly two million people filed past the open coffin of Pope John Paul II when he lay in state in St. Peter's Basilica. The press and television broadcast everywhere the face of the dead pope. The world recognized in his death and funeral a most moving expression and summary of his life as a whole.

For John Paul II and for all of us human beings, death is not an odd fate that comes "from the outside" and strikes us down. We begin dying right from the beginning of our lives. Death is already present in our birth. As the Welsh poet Dylan Thomas said of his own birth, "In the groin of the natural doorway, I crouched like a tailor, sewing a shroud for a journey." His mother gave birth to him "astride the grave." To adapt some words of St. Paul, we live dying and dying we live (2 Cor 6:9). And as Tennessee Williams put it, life "is saturated with death."

Death belongs to life, with every phase of life passing away and with every gain bringing some corresponding loss. Death belongs to each instant and fleeting second of our existence, as the present moment slips into the past. The reality of life is here and now, but we experience this "here and now" as constantly dying and anticipating the definitive closure of biological death. Time runs away from us like sand slipping through our fingers. Relentlessly and inexorably, everything passes.

There is a "once and for all" quality in every day and every moment of our existence. The Letter to the Hebrews declares: "It is appointed for human beings to die once" (9:27). We can press this thought further: We live each day once and for all, and so we might say, "It is appointed for us to live this day once." Lived once and for all, this day can never be changed. Every day of our lives is a little death; it is irreversible and unchangeable. Once lived through, it can never be altered. With life constantly dissolving and escaping from us, we suffer dying even on the way to our final death.

But what of death itself? Who among us can report the experience of death? Of course, there are plausible reports of near-death experiences. But they are just that—*near*-death experiences. Who has experienced death itself and come back to tell us of that experience?

In the village of Castel Gandolfo outside Rome, where popes have their summer residence, a cemetery clings to the slope of a hill. A road sign leading down to it reads: "Cemetery. One-way street." People can return from wars, flights into space, and very remote parts of our globe and tell us what it was like. No one returns from death to tell us what it is like. It is *the* one-way street.

Jesus brought several people back to life: the daughter of Jairus (Mark 5:35–43, with parallels in Matt and Luke); the son of the widow of Nain (Luke 7:11–17); and Lazarus (John 11:38–44). But none of the Gospels ever report what these three people had to say about the experience of death. In the Easter stories, we read of the risen Jesus appearing and commissioning his disciples for the mission to the world that they are to undertake with the power of the Holy Spirit. However, none of the Gospels ever report that Jesus told his followers what it was like to die, to be dead, and then to be raised from the dead.

There is something weirdly alien and disturbingly mysterious about death. We know *that* it is, but we do not know *what* it is. Modern medicine has made some stunning advances and can now describe for us "from the inside" all manner of functions and dysfunctions of our human bodies. But it cannot tell us what *death* is like "from the inside." Death remains an embarrassing mystery for human thought.

Death is mysterious. It is also a solitary affair. We share our living with many other people, but not our dying. In death we are pitilessly alone and in the process of being separated from human society. Death can come in an indefinite variety of ways: through accidents, sudden heart attacks, the gradual collapse of our body's systems through old age, cancer, and other deadly diseases. We may die in a hospital bed surrounded by family members, alone at night in our own bed, or "on stage," so to speak, with all the world to see. In November 1963, President

John Kennedy died a very public death—cradled in his wife's arms. Yet, however and wherever it happens, death is always strangely private: something that happens to "this" one person alone and that shuts down forever "this" individual's story.

These reflections on death are in no way meant to encourage readers to dwell morbidly on their coming end. But sheer common sense agrees with what we read in Thomas à Kempis's *Imitation of Christ*: "If at any time you have seen someone die, acknowledge that you must also pass the same way" (1.23). Visitors to the church of Santa Maria Novella in Florence will not easily forget the words at the foot of Masaccio's masterly portrayal of the crucifixion. A skeleton tells the viewer: "What you are I once was. What I am you one day will be." Realism demands not a morbid obsession with death but a steady awareness that, whatever we do or fail to do in life, our human story will be closed by death.

In the funeral Mass for Pope John Paul II and its concluding rites, there were numerous touching moments. For many of us, the most moving episode came right at the end, when the coffin bearers raised the simple wooden coffin from the ground in front of the altar and carried John Paul II slowly and solemnly along the rows of presidents, monarchs, princes, prime ministers, and other powerful political leaders of our world. As he was being borne past all those celebrities who enjoy lives of pomp and circumstance, it was as if the late pope were preaching his last sermon to them and saying: "You too are mortal. You too must all face death and go home to God."

7

Ash Wednesday

Years ago, I met a man who told me that he knew only one thing about Christians. It was something two of his friends at work did once a year. "They both go off together at lunch hour," he told me, "and when they come back, they have a little ash on their foreheads." What his friends did once a year was to go into a church on Ash Wednesday and receive the ashes.

Around the world on Ash Wednesday, millions of Catholics and some other Christians do the same thing. A priest will sprinkle a little ash on their foreheads and say the words, "Remember you are dust and unto dust you will return."

Ash on our foreheads shows us what we are: people of dust and destined to die. Dust stands for death and for things that break up. Dust is not like the beautiful rocks we can dig up on mountainsides or the lovely seashells we find along the shore. One speck of dust is just like another; it doesn't belong anywhere. It's barely visible and hardly noticeable.

In a way we are all like that: mortal human beings heading toward death. Our lives can seem pointless and meaningless, like dust about to be blown away.

An Arab friend once said to me: "Our lives begin as a drop of seed sown in desire, and end as a handful of dust." Thinking that way about the start of life is a good reminder of how fragile we really are. Why am I here at all? My mother and father need never have met. Circumstances could so easily have been different and never brought them together. Six years into their marriage, without going into biological details, another human being could have emerged to take his or her place in the world, but that new person need not have been me. I need never have existed.

We are all Ash Wednesday people. We exist between a drop of seed sown in desire and a handful of dust about to be blown away.

Probably this is the last thing any us want to be told when we are fit and healthy. I can just hear the voice of my sister-in-law saying, "Gerry, would you please be cheerful and say something positive."

Now I'm all for being positive. After all God is extremely cheerful and very positive, too. But God is also realistic. We too must be realistic and come to terms with what we are.

Death is as important as birth. However, we are not just little piles of dust waiting to finally be blown away on the wind. We are much, much more than that, because God loves each one of us and loves us all with an infinite and faithful love.

—·—·—·—·—·—·—·—·—

8

Seeing Myself

Most of us look at ourselves in a mirror several times a day, when brushing our teeth, combing our hair, applying makeup, or shaving the overnight growth on our face. What would it be like to put a mirror in front of our minds and hearts? What would be seen if the face of our "real" selves were reflected in a mirror?

We might look at our real selves from three angles: as we ourselves see that real self, as other human beings see it, and as God sees it. These three points of view do not always coincide.

(1) Who and what is my "self" as *I* see it? I know that person, don't I? Maybe as a person who is often misunderstood and underappreciated? This or that colleague in the office seems to be down on this person, and it's difficult to know why. They may imagine that this person, who is me, doesn't do as much work as I should. They seem to think that I am lethargic or even a slacker, when the fact is that, at times, I'm just a little tired. That's all.

The people who work in nearby offices are not much better. Some of them appear to have the idea that I am greedy about my food, or that I lose my temper easily—which, of course, is a perfectly ridiculous thing to say.

Perhaps I'm no genius, but I'm really good on the practical side of life. Generally speaking, I am very good-natured and can enjoy a good joke. Maybe I think of myself as very interesting, perhaps even a fascinating sort of person.

(2) Then there is myself and yourself as other people see us. Curiously, that is not quite the same thing. Have you ever overheard some chance remark or criticism that you were not meant to catch, and got a glimpse of what other people think about you? Probably you didn't even hear anything very negative or damaging. But somehow what other people say about us can be very different from what we think about ourselves.

(3) Finally, there is the third point of view—yourself as God sees you. It is the self as reflected in the divine mirror that matters most. What should most concern and encourage us is what God thinks of us, rather than what we think of ourselves or what others think of us. God knows our real self far better than

even we do. God sees not only our sins, our weaknesses, and our excuses, but also our inner selves, "the hidden person of the heart" and its precious, lasting beauty that God finds and loves (1 Pet 3:4).

Of course, we never see that "hidden person" of our hearts reflected in our bathroom mirrors. But God does. God knows that hidden self to be full of possibilities and truly beautiful.

God, who is "closer to us than we are to ourselves" (St. Augustine), looks at us from the most significant angle. It is the divine viewpoint on our real self that should challenge and hearten us far more than the viewpoint that anyone else ever takes. We can only pray for the privilege and grace to share a little in what God sees us to be and to accept what God wants to see us become.

Sin

1. Sins of others
2 legalistic v revelation
3 easy way out
4. Omission
5. Mystery — failure to love

9

Sin

"Then he began to reproach the cities in which most of his deeds of power had been done, because they did not repent" (Matt 11:20). Jesus' words give rise to pointed questions: *Why* don't we repent of our sins? What stops us from repenting and truly hearing the good news that is Jesus himself? Why do we find it hard to face and acknowledge our sins? We might come up with several reasons by way of an answer.

First, it is a lot easier to notice the sins of others rather than our own. We can be very good at noticing the sins of our next-door neighbor and perhaps even better at noticing the sins of church leaders, politicians, and lawyers. The prophet Nathan took advantage of our sharp eye for the faults of others by telling David a story about a rich man stealing a lamb that belonged to a poor man. David became instantly indignant about this injustice, and only then came to recognize his own terrible sin of murder and adultery (2 Sam 12:1–15).

Second, we may fail to acknowledge and repent of our sins because we have fallen into the habit of looking upon sin simply as a failure to measure up to some law. Here are the regulations and we have not met the required standards. How annoying! I've spoiled my track record! But sin is not simply spoiling our record or failing to fulfill some regulation. Sin means a major or minor breakdown in personal relations with God and with our fellow human beings. The Ten Commandments, besides showing us a true road map for living, repeatedly suggest that sin involves a breakdown in our personal relationship with God and with other men and women.

Third, we don't recognize and express remorse for our sins because sin is often an easy way out. It can seem so much easier to miss Mass, to follow others in unjust practices, and to cheat on our marriage partners—easier than getting up on a cold morning, bucking the tide, or remaining faithful. Consciously or unconsciously, we may be reluctant to face up to and stop doing things that have regularly offered us an easy way out.

Fourth, many sins are things we *fail* to do: sins of omission. It is less difficult to admit and be sorry for sins of commission (the bad things we have actually done) than to repent of sins of omission. In the verse previously quoted from Matthew's Gospel, Jesus was reproaching the people of several cities for what they had failed to do. He was in their midst, working miracles and preaching his message of God's saving mercy, but somehow they missed the point. They were not up to recognizing the precious, once-and-for-all chance they were being offered. They failed to acknowledge Jesus for what he was: the unique and literal "God-send" that would bring them nothing but peace and lasting joy.

Fifth, a final reason why it may be difficult to recognize and repent of our sins comes from the strange nature of sin itself. Like love itself, sin as a failure to love is mysterious, even deeply mysterious. More than something clearly intelligible to our minds, sin and love come from our hearts. The heart has its "reasons," for good or evil, for what it does and for what it fails to do.

We can only pray for the courage to recognize not only our sinfulness but also the "God-send" that Jesus is. He is the love of God in person, the one who wants to take away our sins and fill our hearts forever.

10

"...for what we have failed to do"

When human beings fail in love, that can often mean their refusal to commit, to care about the needs of others, and even just to get involved.

In his famous parable on the last judgment of all humanity (Matt 25:31–46), Jesus pictured a separation of human beings into two classes, the sheep and the goats. The separation turned simply on the question of whether or not they had rendered a service of love to those in distress. Had they fed the hungry, welcomed the stranger, clothed the naked, taken care of the sick, and visited prisoners?

It would be going too far to say that such service of love is the *only* point on which people will be judged. But the service of love is clearly the chief point of judgment; it gathers up the entire code of human and Christian conduct. It is not that commandments prohibiting theft, murder, and adultery are made optional or even cancelled. However, it seems to be assumed that those who take the initiative in loving their neighbors in distress will also not steal, murder, or cheat on their spouses. Those who show hospitality to the stranger, kindness to the sick, and practical concern for the jailed will presumably be truthful, honest in business matters, faithful in marriage, and regular in personal prayer and in the public worship of God.

In that scenario of the last judgment, everything hinges on the willingness to become involved. In the case of those who, for one reason or another, have failed to become involved, nothing is said about their sins of commission. It all turns on what they have failed to do, their sins of omission.

This scene of judgment has two striking counterparts in Luke's Gospel: the story of the Good Samaritan (Luke 10:29–37) and the story of the rich man and Lazarus (Luke 16:19–31). Unlike the priest and Levite who refuse to cross the road and help a badly wounded traveler, the Good Samaritan gets involved. He spends his time and his money in caring for someone he comes across who's in terrible distress.

In the story about the rich man and Lazarus, there is not the slightest suggestion that the rich man had stolen money or in other ways had gained his wealth dishonestly. He failed because he spent his time carousing with family and friends, and ignored the needs of a starving beggar right there at his gate.

The judgment scene in Matthew and the two stories in Luke raise the painful question: What are the things that *I* fail to do for those in need?

--- --- --- --- --- ---

11

Surfers, Wanderers, or Pilgrims?

In the first part of this book, we explored various aspects of our human condition. To round off these chapters we might usefully reflect on three images that can express our existence: as surfers, wanderers, or pilgrims.

Surfers try to work out the right spot on the advancing wave and balance themselves there, albeit precariously. The correct balance means not sliding back behind the wave and not facing a fall by being too far out in front. It's all rather like life itself. When the past yields to the present and the future, we try to discern where we should balance ourselves. As surfers on the ocean of human existence, we want to balance ourselves, so that we neither slide back into the past nor rush forward recklessly into the future. For this image of life, discernment and balance are crucial.

For those who prefer the image of a wanderer, years ago Andrew Greeley published a splendid book, *Life for a Wanderer*. To picture human life as wandering, he took up such current expressions as "hang loose," "travel light," and "play it by ear."

One needs flexibility in dealing with what happens. Those who wander will meet unforeseen difficulties, even new difficulties that they have never encountered before. They will also run into unforeseen opportunities. To cope with those difficulties and take advantage of those opportunities, wanderers need to be resilient and resourceful. Greeley put his own vision of *Christian* wandering this way: "We have come a long way and yet there is still a long way to go, but, unlike John Wayne and the other western heroes riding off into the sunset, the light we are wandering toward is the sunrise."

From the time of the New Testament, many Christians interpreted their lives as a journey or pilgrimage toward their heavenly homeland. Famously Dante Alighieri used the pilgrimage theme in his *Divine Comedy*. In that work, the spiritual transformation of the pilgrim takes him through hell and purgatory to heaven. In the Middle Ages, pilgrimages to Jerusalem, Rome, Santiago de Compostela, Canterbury, Walsingham, and other shrines strengthened the pilgrim's common faith and sense of life's meaning. At the end of the journey, a venerated sanctuary renewed a deep feeling of being with Christ and his saints. The ancient Celts called such shrines "thin places." Time and again, pilgrims experienced there a close communion among God, themselves, and fellow pilgrims.

In modern times, pilgrimages have enjoyed a huge revival. They reinforce a consciousness of life as a spiritual journey, a preparation for death and eternal life. They sustain a sense of moving through time to finally meeting God.

Whether we like or not, life never stands still. We are all going places. That leaves us with two questions: Do I think of myself as a surfer, a wanderer, or a pilgrim? Who is my most treasured companion on that journey?

Part Two

Jesus in
His Lifetime

1

Jesus, Our Friend

We come now to two questions: Who is Jesus? What has he done and what is he doing for us? Here many reach instinctively for the theme of Jesus, Our Friend. In John's Gospel, Jesus tells his followers: "I have called you friends" (John 15:15). A vivid sense of Jesus as our "friend" began to flourish among Christians after the year 1000, when a heightened sensitivity to the humanity of Jesus emerged, along with a new openness to deeply felt personal relationships. As St. Aelred, the abbot of Rievaulx in Yorkshire, put it, a friend "is the best medicine in life."

A widespread interest in the Song of Songs encouraged very affectionate language in talking to and about Jesus: our mother, lover, and friend. A prayer by St. Richard of Chichester captures the new tenderness: "Thanks be to thee, my Lord Jesus Christ, for all the benefits which thou hast given me—for all the pains and insults thou hast borne for me. O most merciful Redeemer, Friend, and Brother, may I know thee more clearly, love thee more dearly, and follow thee more nearly."

Christian faith brings a call to identify with and give our whole lives to this friend. Yet he is a friend whom we never see, or at least never see directly. He is a friend who is with us all our days, albeit invisibly present. But the Gospels fill out for us the story of what he was like and, in particular, what it cost Jesus to live out his loving friendship toward us.

It is not that he literally underwent every possible form of human suffering or took on every possible form of human toil on our behalf. Rather, he accepted the human condition with all the inevitable pains that it involved, and dedicated himself totally to a mission for God's kingdom, which brought him much distress and lethal danger.

Before Jesus began his ministry, he went into the desert for forty days of prayer and fasting. Once his ministry started, he gave himself to it unconditionally. On one occasion he became so exhausted that he fell asleep in a boat and slept through a storm (Mark 4:35–41). He suffered the hurtful outrage of hearing his acts of deliverance attributed to the power of the ruler of demons (Mark 3:22–27). He felt the sting of failure, as he saw his best efforts to reform the religious life of Jerusalem going for nothing. He wept over this city, which had not recognized in his mission "the things that made for peace" (Luke 19:41–44). Judas, one of his closest disciples, betrayed him. The leader of his "core group," Simon Peter, protested that he would face death with Jesus. But a few hours later, Peter swore an oath that he didn't even know him (Mark 14:31, 71). Jesus was terribly let down by those on whom he thought he could rely.

At the end, Jesus experienced awful fear and loneliness. In the Garden of Gethsemane, he became deeply "distressed and agitated." He reproached Peter, James, and John for falling asleep and failing to provide some comfort when fear and panic swept over him: "Could you not watch one hour with me?" (Mark 14:32–42).

The religious authorities and Pilate set justice aside as they joined forces to condemn Jesus to death. He was scourged, mocked, and then crucified on Calvary, the "place of the skull."

He died there like a criminal, nailed to a cross and flanked by criminals.

When we gaze at our friend on the cross, we might well accept the invitation from St. Ignatius Loyola in his *Spiritual Exercises* and ask ourselves: "What have I done for Christ? What am I doing for Christ? What ought I to do for Christ?"

In the *Dies irae* ("day of wrath"), a hymn used for centuries at Masses for the dead, one verse recalls Christ sitting weary and worn out. A close translation of the Latin, rather than the rhymed verse that might be more familiar, is this: "Seeking me you sat down tired out; you redeemed me having endured the cross; may such labor not be in vain" ("Quaerens me sedisti lassus; redemisti crucem passus; tantus labor non sit cassus").

Some simple lines that I picked up in Hong Kong put these same sentiments into a contemporary setting and the gestures made by rich nations toward the poor of this world:

> God did not send into our tormented world technical aid, Gabriel with a group of experts. He did not send food nor discarded clothes of angels. Even less, did he extend long-term loans? Rather, he came himself, [was] born in a stable, starved in a desert, [died] naked on a cross. And sharing with us, he became our food; and suffering with us, he became our joy.

These are the "headlines" about Jesus. Let us now sample some episodes and some teaching from the Gospels. They can prompt worthwhile answers to the questions: What was and what is Jesus like? What did he do for us, and what does he do for us? Why do we need him, and how does he satisfy our deepest desires?

2

The Beauty of Jesus

S everal years ago some scientists at a British university published the results of their research into the way newborn babies react to beautiful music and beautiful faces. The babies seemed persistently happy with the melodic strains of Vivaldi's *Four Seasons*. But they became disturbed by the same work when it was played backward. The babies also turned away from ugly faces and showed a marked preference for people with beautiful faces.

From their research, the scientists drew the conclusion that we are born with an innate sense of beauty. Nature has programmed us to find beauty attractive, whether it is a matter of beautiful music or beautiful people. Maybe this piece of scientific research simply proves what many people already know intuitively.

It is in our human makeup to be attracted by beauty. Beautiful things and beautiful people have an instant and deep impact on us. We fall in love with those who are beautiful; we want to sing their praises and stay in their presence.

In the story of the marriage feast at Cana (John 2:1–11), we hear that through the miracle of changing water into wine Jesus revealed his glory. In the scriptures "glory," God's radiant glory, is very close in meaning to beauty. To say then that Jesus revealed his glory, his radiant splendor, is tantamount to saying that he disclosed his beauty.

Right through John's Gospel, we meet this major theme: Jesus manifested his luminous beauty. In the opening chapter, John writes: "The Word became flesh and dwelt amongst us, and we saw his glory" (John 1:14). This amounts to saying: "We saw, we contemplated, his beauty." In a very real sense, the whole of John's Gospel is one long act of contemplation, the contemplation of the beauty of Christ.

And that is the way Jesus saves us. He reveals his glorious beauty to us, and we have the chance of falling in love with him, staying in love with him, and sharing in that inexhaustible fullness of "grace and truth" that he brings us (John 1:14, 16).

The great Russian novelist Fyodor Dostoevsky declared: "It is beauty that will save the world." I would dare to add: "It is beauty that is already saving the world." Beauty opens our eyes and enables us to see the truth. Beauty helps us to live up to what we know to be good. Without beauty to focus our lives, things can seem meaningless and even absurd.

Falling in love with a beautiful person, whether inwardly beautiful or outwardly beautiful, liberates people from their chaotic wanderings. It can bring order and direction into their lives. We have all known persons whose existence was transformed when they fell in love with a beautiful person or a beautiful project.

Small children, even newborn babies, can tell us what we human beings are really like. We are drawn to beauty. We love beauty. We are changed and even transformed by it.

The beautiful Christ wants to reveal his uniquely glorious beauty to each one of us. Whenever that happens, we will be drawn to love him. His radiant beauty will snatch away our hearts and so shape our whole existence, now and forever. Nothing can transform a human life more happily and permanently than a deep experience of Jesus' radiant beauty.

3

Being Sentimental at Christmas

Many years ago, only a few months after my ordination, I helped in a parish from the middle of Advent through to the New Year. As Christmas approached, I became full of doubts about introducing a particular story into my homily. It seemed almost too sentimental, and I felt embarrassed at the thought that some friend or relative might be there in church to hear me preach on Christmas Day. Let me summarize the story, so that readers will understand why I hesitated about using it.

Once upon a time, a nun was telling her class of small boys and girls the story of the birth of Jesus. The nun naturally began with Mary and Joseph coming along the road from Nazareth to Bethlehem during the winter. When they arrived, they tried a hotel but found that it was booked out. The manager suggested a place up the road. They tried there too and it was the same story: "I'm terribly sorry but there's no room available." Finally, someone told them about a cave up on the slope of the hillside. So they climbed up there to the cave, which had been used to house farm animals. The nun described the cave. It had no door; the wind blew in. The cave itself was damp, dirty, and cold. She went on to tell the boys and girls how Jesus was born in that cave. "Now," she asked them. "What would you have done if you had been there in the cave with Jesus, Mary, and Joseph?"

One little boy shot his hand up and said: "Sister, I would have taken a broom and swept the cave clean." A little girl told the nun: "Sister, I would have made three cups of coffee: one for Mary, one for Joseph, and one for Jesus." A second little boy had his answer: "I would have taken my jacket off and put it around baby Jesus." Another little boy told the nun: "I would have gathered some wood and made a big fire." And so the answers went on until, finally, the nun noticed that everyone had said something except for the smallest child who sat at the back of the class. "Helen," she asked, "what would you have done?" "Sister," the little girl said in a whisper, "if Mary would have let me, I would have taken the baby into my arms and just loved him." That, of course, was the best answer of all. Love is what Jesus wants from us. Our love is the only thing that will satisfy him.

So I told that story in my Christmas homily and went on to apply it to the congregation in front of me:

At Christmas what Jesus wants from us is not some effort to clean up a dirty cave, or to provide a cup of warm coffee, a thick jacket, or a cheerful fire. What he wants is our love. At Christmas, one of the best ways to show our love is by making a very loving and well-prepared confession and communion.

In the last few weeks we made out our lists of people whom we wanted to give presents to or at least send Christmas cards to. But let's not forget that Christmas is Our Lord's birthday. Don't let us leave his name off our lists. Don't let Christmas pass without remembering to give him our love. There could hardly be a better way of giving him our love than by meeting him through an extra special confession and communion. We can make that confession and communion extra special by going and kneeling for a while in front of the Christmas crib and remembering the love that drove him to come among us long ago as a tiny baby that first Christmas.

That was what I preached in my first Christmas homily after ordination. As it happened, none of my relatives or friends was present, but there happened to be a man at Mass who had spent years alienated from faith and the practice of faith. He underwent a dramatic conversion that Christmas Day. He was a total stranger to me and I never saw him again. However, I learned afterward that, in God's good providence, my sentimental story of the nun teaching her little children about Christmas touched his heart and opened him up to the grace of God. So, there could be a place for sentimental stories in Christmas homilies. To understate matters enormously, God did something rather sentimental by coming among us as a tiny child. Sharing in the whole messy experience of being human was a very sentimental thing for God to do.

4

Christos the King

During the twentieth century, the English-speaking world was blessed by a number of outstanding Christian authors. I am thinking of writers like G. K. Chesterton, Dorothy Day, T. S. Eliot, C. S. Lewis, Thomas Merton, Dorothy Sayers, and J. R. R. Tolkien. Dorothy Sayers published detective stories. But during the Second World War, she also wrote for the BBC a remarkable cycle of radio plays on the life of Christ. She gave that cycle of plays the title of *The Man Born to Be King*.

The first play, which was broadcast in December 1941, features the three wise men and their visit to King Herod the Great. When Balthazar and the other two wise men meet the king, they tell him that they are looking for Jesus, the newborn King of the Jews. Herod looks puzzled and says to them, I'm quoting now: "You speak mysteries. Tell me this: will he be a warrior king?"

Balthazar replies: "The greatest of warriors. Yet he shall be called the Prince of Peace. He will be victor and victim in all his wars, and will make his triumph in defeat. And when the wars are over, he'll rule his people with love."

Herod, however, is not convinced and tells Balthazar: "You can't rule men with love. When you find your king, tell him so." The old tyrant goes on to explain his policy: "Only three things will govern a people—fear and greed and the promise of security. Don't I know it!…I've been a stern ruler—dreaded and hated—and yet my country is prosperous and her borders at peace."

Then Herod adds bitterly: "But wherever I loved, I found treachery—wife, children, brother—all of them, all of them. Love is a traitor; it has betrayed me; it betrays all kings. It will betray your Christ. Give him that message from Herod, King of the Jews."

You know, it's not just old King Herod in a play by Dorothy Sayers who gives us that message. Plenty of people will tell you that the only way to run the world is through fear, greed, and the promise of security. Plenty of people will tell you that love is a traitor that finally betrays us all.

But they are wrong. Love is stronger than fear and greed. It's stronger than any worries about security, whether it's the security of our country or the security of our personal lives. True peace comes through love, not through being afraid of one another and greedily protecting our own interests at all costs, as old King Herod did.

Jesus is the Prince of Peace, the King of Peace. He loves us and helps us to love one another. Give his love half a chance and you will find peace, real peace, the kind of peace that no one can ever take from you. Give his love half a chance, and you will know a security that will never, ever end.

Balthazar was right. On the cross, Jesus looked like a victim, a hopelessly defeated victim. But he turned out to be the victor, the one who triumphed when it really mattered at the end. He rules now with love. Give his love a real chance in your lives, a really big chance in your lives.

Jesus was and is the man born to be King—the true and lasting King in the lives of all of us. It is only this King who pours out his love on us, both in this life and in the next.

—·—·—·—·—·—·—

5

The Baptism of Jesus

The story of Jesus' baptism (Matt 3:13–17) is an amazing scenario. Picture it: At the bottom, you see Jesus coming out of the waters of the river Jordan. Above him, the heavens are opened and the Holy Spirit descends on him in the form of a dove. Right at the top, a voice sounds out from heaven, saying: "This is my beloved Son, with whom I am well pleased."

It is an extraordinary scenario: the voice of the Father ringing out above, the Spirit coming down under the appearance of a dove, and the beloved Son of God emerging from the waters of the Jordan. In the Gospel of Matthew, this is a unique scene, featuring the tripersonal God. The heavens open up, and God is revealed to us as Father, Son, and Holy Spirit.

Matthew begins the story of Jesus' work on earth by putting before us a sensational tableau: the self-manifestation of God as three-in-one. What follows in this Gospel will develop and unfold this picture from the baptism of Jesus: the picture of God disclosed as Father, Son, and Holy Spirit. The picture at the start of Matthew's Gospel sums up everything that will follow. *This is our God*, the God who is three-in-one.

But why is this revelation uniquely important? What difference would it make if God were simply one, not three-in-one, and not revealed as Father, Son, and Holy Spirit? The astonishing heart of what was revealed at Jesus' baptism is this: God is a holy family; God is *the* holy family, the Three-in-One who live together in an ecstatic communion of love.

One of the most remarkable modern hymns to the Trinity is Brian Wren's "How Wonderful the Three-in-One," a hymn that sings of their "communing love in shared delight." Those words apply beautifully to the ecstatic life the Father, Son, and Holy Spirit have shared together from all eternity. They live with one another and *for* one another in an infinite ecstasy of love.

This divine holy family shows all of us what to do with our lives and how to let our lives become an existence of communing love. The holy family that is the Blessed Trinity forms *the* central role model for human life. We lose nothing but receive everything by sharing in that divine love, a divine love that wants everyone to be a winner and no one to be a loser.

Seen this way, the picture with which Matthew opens his story of Jesus' ministry is a matter of life and death for all of us. Matthew shows us the Three-in-One, our God who calls us to take part in that communion of rapturous love that is the heart of the divine life.

Yes, God is communing love in shared delight. May we all allow ourselves to be drawn more and more into that communing love. May we all experience ever more deeply how wonderful is our God, the Three-in-One revealed at the baptism of Jesus.

6

Three Beatitudes

On four occasions, from 1996 to 2003, I cochaired conferences on four basic Christian beliefs: the resurrection, the Trinity, the incarnation, and the redemption. Specialists in various disciplines, the scholars who presented papers belonged to different Christian churches, but all shared the central Creed recited or sung around the world every Sunday.

The fourth and final symposium reflected on the redemption that Jesus has brought for all of us. One very striking contribution examined what some famous modern writers have said,—explicitly or, more often, implicitly—about human redemption.

What emerged clearly from this paper was the recurrent temptation for self-reliance, the temptation to understand life as saving ourselves. In this widespread view, our existence offers the chance of a "do-it-yourself" salvation.

That's all very different from the program that Jesus announced in his Beatitudes: "Blessed are the poor in spirit; theirs is the kingdom of heaven. Blessed are those who mourn; they shall be comforted. Blessed are those who hunger and thirst for what is right; they shall be satisfied" (Matt 5:3–4, 6). Luke puts these same Beatitudes more directly, using "you" rather than "they": "Blessed are you poor, for yours is the kingdom of God. Blessed are you who weep now, for you shall laugh. Blessed are you that hunger now, for you shall be satisfied" (Luke 6:20–21).

These three Beatitudes are very simple, stark, laconic. Jesus declares to be happy and blessed those who are poor, those who mourn and weep, and those who hunger and thirst. Their situation, he promises, will be reversed by God; they will be fed to the full by God.

The Beatitudes present people in great distress and in situations that they have not chosen for themselves—situations about which they can do little or nothing. They seem vulnerable and powerless, but God's promise is held out to them. They *will* enjoy the kingdom of heaven, they *will* be consoled, and they *will* be utterly satisfied.

What catches the eye is that, according to the Beatitudes, the end results are not said to depend on one's commitment to Jesus, let alone on one's performance. Jesus does not say: "Blessed are you poor who are my faithful disciples." Nor does he say: "Blessed are those loyal followers of mine who weep now and suffer from hunger." Jesus simply delivers a promise to those in real distress: "God will bring to an end the present painful state of affairs, not because of your achievements or your loyalty to me, but simply because you are suffering."

The Lord knows how many terribly painful states of affairs afflict the whole world and the people of our own country. Innumerable people have no redress and suffer in situations that they have not chosen for themselves.

Through Jesus, God makes an unconditional promise, or at least a promise that carries no explicit conditions and has no strings attached. Jesus does not tell us: "Blessed are the poor who are always faithful to God." Nor does he tell us: "Blessed are those who weep and hunger now who always keep the divine commandments."

There is no question of such people having some strict claim on God. They cannot insist on what they deserve or on what they think their achievements have merited. Rather, these three Beatitudes show us God's gratuitous, loving, and powerful mercy, a mercy that God simply extends to those in painful need and distress. God cares deeply about powerless and vulnerable people, and will reverse their situation. God will comfort and satisfy them.

These Beatitudes sum up vivid parables preached by Jesus, like that of the Prodigal Son (Luke 15:11–32) and that of the Pharisee and the Tax Collector (Luke 18:9–14). Those two parables set before us human beings in desperate need. These persons are not good or virtuous, but simply persons in great need. Through God's loving kindness, they receive what they cannot claim to have earned.

That is what those two parables are about and what our three Beatitudes express in summary form. God will vindicate the poor, the mourners, and the hungry. These and other suffering people desperately need help, and God will supply it.

The Beatitudes summarize Jesus' proclamation of the divine kingdom. They are the heart of his message. In the three Beatitudes that I have highlighted, Jesus shows us what God promises to those in pain. Jesus invites us to share his vision of a suffering and fearful world. God cares unconditionally for those who suffer.

How blessed we will be if we really share the vision of Jesus and find through the Beatitudes the secret of life, the secret of the only life truly worth living.

- - - - - - - - - - - - - - - - -

7

The First Beatitude

A s we saw in the last chapter, there is a difference between the way Matthew and Luke report the first Beatitude. Luke simply reports Jesus as saying: "Blessed are you poor." Matthew has: "Blessed are the poor in spirit."

Matthew wants us to remember an Old Testament nuance that supplies the background to what Jesus says. The *anawim*, or poor in spirit, are those who are unjustly deprived of their rights and goods. Old Testament prophets, psalms, and books frequently evoke the situation of the impoverished, the sorrowful, the helpless, and all those whose rights God promises to vindicate. They can trust in God, because God will lift them out of their wretched state.

God will come to their aid, not because they deserve divine help but simply because they are desperately in need and no one except God can or will supply help. We have a spectacular example of what the first Beatitude means: St. Josephine Bakhita.

Josephine was born in Darfur, a region of the Sudan, which has often been in the news recently because of the awful sufferings of its people. As a little girl, Josephine went through the trauma of having her sister carried off by slave traders. In a subsequent raid, she herself was carried off and sold into slavery. Her first owner called her *Bakhita*, meaning "lucky." But she was anything but lucky, since a succession of owners treated her cruelly. Later she said about that time: "A hidden power within me sustained me." When she came to know this power as God, she added: "If I were to spend my whole life on my knees, I could not thank the good God enough."

Bakhita's last owner was an official at the Italian consulate in Khartoum. When he and his family returned to Italy to settle near Venice, Bakhita went with them. She enrolled in a catechumenate program conducted by the Canossian Sisters, and in January 1890 received the sacraments of baptism, confirmation, and first communion. Three years later, she joined the sisters to live the religious life for forty-four years. She passed her time in sewing, cooking, looking after the chapel, and answering the door.

Noticing Josephine's ever-deepening absorption in the spirit of the Beatitudes, the community became more and more convinced that they had a saint among them. So too were the people of the town where she lived. After her death in 1947, this conviction deepened and was vindicated in 1992 when John Paul II declared her blessed and in 2000 when he declared her a saint. Josephine is now known throughout the Catholic world and beyond to be not merely "lucky" but to be truly "blessed" — Bakhita blessed by God.

I don't know any other modern story that translates more strikingly that first Beatitude: "Blessed are the poor in spirit, for theirs is the kingdom of God."

Of course, several of the subsequent Beatitudes are going to invite us to live in new ways and practice a certain kind of life: "Blessed are the meek; blessed are the merciful; blessed are the pure of heart; blessed are the peacemakers." Jesus wants us to be meek, people who humbly admit our total dependence on God and living with others in a nonviolent way. Jesus wants us to be merciful, people who forgive those who trespass against us. Jesus wants us to be clean of heart, people who stand before God with utter honesty and integrity. Jesus wants us to be people who spread peace in the world.

Yes, the full list of Beatitudes also includes a program of things for which we should take responsibility, things that we should faithfully practice because we accept from Jesus the full message of God's kingdom. But before the Beatitudes start sketching our responsibilities, they highlight the gift of God, the largeness of God's heart. God, Jesus assures us, cares deeply and lovingly about all people in need and distress. Blessed are the poor; blessed are those who mourn and weep—for they have God on their side.

———————————————

8

"Love your enemies; do good to those who hate you"

Some of you or maybe many of you, Dear Readers, will have read sections from the writings of St. Thomas Aquinas, or perhaps even whole works by him. Every one of you, I imagine, will at least have heard of him.

Thomas Aquinas deserves all the praise he has received as one of the great Christian thinkers of all time. Here I want to praise him, not so much for his brilliance of thought, but for his realism. He was very realistic about human beings and the human condition. He spent, for example, pages and pages reflecting on hatred. Human beings do hate each other. That's a sad reality in our world. It is very sad to see the amount of hatred that can exist between individuals, between groups of people, between nations, and between religions.

In facing up to hatred, Aquinas proved himself very like Jesus. The Gospels show Jesus to have been realistic in his teaching: "Love your enemies; do good to those who hate you" (Luke 6:27). There *are* people who hate us and curse us. We *do* have enemies. And in return, we too can hate people and feel like cursing them and doing them harm, or at least feel like not doing them any good.

Of course, we can be tempted to deny that: "I don't have any enemies. Everyone loves me, or at least everyone likes me. There is no one that I hate. Oh yes, there are people I avoid and try never to meet. But I don't hate them. It's just that I prefer the company of others." With these or other words, we can go into denial about enemies and hatred.

Yet Jesus simply takes it for granted that we do have enemies and that hatred is something we all need to struggle with. Centuries after the time of Jesus, Thomas Aquinas took it for granted that hatred haunts our world and that we do have our enemies. We don't face the issue or solve the problem by denying it. Aquinas and, even more, Jesus himself, would shake his head over us if we tried to claim that there is no hatred in our lives and that there are no enemies around to detest us.

But what should we do about our enemies? Jesus is extremely practical. He doesn't offer some general advice, like "love your enemies," and leave it at that. He presses on to make clear what the practice of love demands. It means blessing and praying for our enemies, no hitting back at them violently when they treat us badly or rob us. "Love your enemies" means for-giving them. It even means going out of our way to do them good. What Jesus spells out in detail about the practice of loving our enemies is fiercely challenging (Luke 6:28–38). But he does make his challenge, and he makes it to everyone who is willing to listen to him.

Look at two things Jesus lists in his practice of loving our enemies: doing good and showing forgiveness. First, doing good. As Jesus remarks, we can drift into the habit of doing good to those who do good to us. It is not that hard to do good to people who are generous and kind to us. In fact, we may think of this as a wise investment. Here are these people who do us good. If we show them only a bit of kindness, they may be even more generous toward us. But reaching out and doing good to our *enemies*? That's another question. Reaching out in love to our enemies can seem like walking through open ground under gunfire. It's something we don't like doing, and it can be very risky. Real love always makes us vulnerable and liable to being hurt. Loving our enemies makes us especially vulnerable. Yet, that is what Jesus asks of us.

And then forgiveness. Jesus puts that down on the list of things that real love for our enemies must include. "Forgive," he says, "and you will be forgiven." It's an interesting and suggestive fact that in many modern languages "for-give" is a strengthened form of "give": for instance, *par-donner* (French), *ver-geben* (Geman), *per-donare* (Italian), and *per-donar* (Spanish). Language itself seems to imply that "for-giving" means "giving and giving, even giving and giving and giving an indefinite number of times. It can sometimes prove hard to give; it is always harder, even much harder, to forgive.

In this section of Luke's Gospel (with its parallels in Matthew's Sermon on the Mount), Jesus proposes a most chal-lenging, even terrifying, program. He asks us to forgive our enemies and go out of our way to do them good. The extreme and even costly nature of what Jesus asks certainly justifies G. K. Chesterton's famous quip: "Christianity hasn't been tried and found wanting. It has been found hard and not tried."

How can we cope with Jesus' challenge? How can we take a plunge and start loving and forgiving our enemies, *even* our enemies, and *especially* our enemies? It certainly helps if we see how Jesus lived exactly what he preached. Our passage from Luke's Gospel describes perfectly the life and practice of Jesus. He loved his enemies and did good to those who hated him. He blessed those who cursed him. He prayed for those who treated him badly. No wonder then that he died praying: "Father, forgive them, for they know not what they do" (Luke 23:34).

Jesus, help us to live out your program of life and love.
Help us to set aside hatred, to forgive our enemies, and to
do good to all.
Make us overcome hatred with love, with your love.

9

Good or Bad Foundations

At the end of the Sermon on the Mount, Jesus introduces the image of a wise man and a foolish man (Matt 7:21–29). Both of them want to build a home for themselves. The wise man builds his house on rock and the foolish man builds his house on sand. And then the wet season comes, with lots of rain and wind, and maybe a flash flood or two. The house built on rock survives it all, but the house built on sand collapses and is swept away.

Some years ago, a young engineer was talking to me about the contrast that Jesus drew between these two builders. My friend pointed out that sand can make an excellent foundation. "Yes," I said to him, "but maybe the problem was that the foolish man built his house in the wrong place, perhaps in a narrow valley, where torrential rainfall could produce sudden, really bad floods."

Whatever precise picture we are meant to imagine, Jesus pushes the tough question at us: What is our life really built on? On the rock of his teaching? Or on something else, something unstable?

We have only one go at life, and Jesus wants us all to make the very best of it. We have the choice of either letting his wisdom shape our lives or letting our lives become misshapen and even collapse through relying on false principles. The stakes are very high: either we allow Jesus to take over our lives, or at our peril, we hang back from that commitment.

It is a stark alternative Jesus proposes: either be a wise person or be a foolish person. We will prove ourselves wise people if we persistently follow his teaching. He is our rock, our fortress, and our strength. What he wants for us is nothing but the very best.

Some time back, the editor of a leading Catholic journal phoned me to seek advice for a talk he had been asked to give to a group of Anglican clergy. "What do you think I should tell them?" he asked. "Tell them to stick close to Jesus," I told him. And I added: "You might want to quote that Evangelical line, 'Put your hand in the hand of the man from Galilee.' For good measure, you might as well say, 'Put your hand in his hand and keep it there.'"

Jesus is the wisest friend any of us can ever have. If we build our lives on him and his teaching, nothing, in the end, can go wrong. If we take his hand, he will lead us along the right path.

Matthew did something wonderful for us by gathering together in the three chapters we call the Sermon on the Mount the key teachings of Jesus. These chapters end in the most challenging way, with the sharp choice between following the example of a wise man or the example of a foolish man.

If we agree with what we hear Jesus saying in the Sermon on the Mount, we must faithfully build our lives on that teaching or, rather, *allow* our lives to be built on that teaching. In Jesus and his teaching, we have the wisest foundation possible for a truly wonderful life, now and forever.

Matthew closes the Sermon on the Mount with this: "When Jesus had finished saying these things, the crowds were astonished at his teaching. For he taught them as one having *authority* and not as their scribes" (Matt 7:28–29).

In his 2007 book, *Jesus of Nazareth*, Pope Benedict XVI gives full space to the Sermon on the Mount. It becomes easily the longest chapter in the book. That chapter contains a very helpful dialogue with an American rabbi, Jacob Neusner. Back in 2000, Neusner published a book that the pope takes up, *A Rabbi Talks with Jesus*. One can well understand how the pope appreciates many things that Neusner has to say; for instance, when the rabbi recognizes that "Jesus' claim to authority is at issue." Neusner goes on to admit: "I now realize that only God can demand of me what Jesus is asking." With great respect Neusner declines to accept Jesus' claim to authority and politely turns away.

Believing Christians have not declined that claim to authority and turned away. At least in theory, they recognize and accept Jesus' claims along with what Jesus asks of them. We all want to say to Jesus with full sincerity: "You are the Lord of my life. Your Sermon on the Mount is my program for living." Yet it is a daunting, almost fearful, matter to live our lives under the authority of someone, even when that someone is Jesus himself. It can be frightening to say to Jesus: "You are my Lord, with authority over my whole life."

When we say that to Jesus, we might remember a word that is connected with "authority," a word that happily recalls what the authority of Jesus means for us and for our lives. *Authority* comes from the Latin *auctoritas*, and that Latin word is connected with a Latin verb, *augere*, which means "to grow." That connection can happily remind us that the authority of Jesus is worlds apart from any power play. His authority aims at *augere*, at making us grow.

All true authority is like that; it aims at making people grow and flourish wonderfully. Yes, it is with ultimate, divine authority that Jesus teaches us and leads us. But his exercise of authority over us has no aim other than to make us truly grow and flourish now and forever. Only God can demand of us what Jesus asks. And what Jesus asks of us with his divine authority is for our full and lasting growth and good.

10

A Question and a Saying

I t was during five years of living in Boston that I celebrated Mass for the first time with a blind priest. Larry presided and took fear as the theme for his homily. He spoke of his own fears in coping with life and work in a new city: "How would I negotiate the trees along the sidewalks? Then there are the streets to cross and the traffic to cope with. How will I know when the bus reaches the hospital where I am to work as chaplain?"

Larry ran through his various fears and then reached his punch line: "One way or another we are all afraid. But Jesus is the One who saves us from our fears and takes our fears away." It was very moving to hear a blind person confessing to his fears and testifying to his rock-hard faith in Jesus.

That homily brought to mind the searching question that Jesus put to his disciples after he had calmed a storm that threatened to swamp their boat: "Why are you afraid?" (Mark 4:40).

We might well extend the question to us and ask: Who are we afraid of? What feeds our fears? We may be frightened of certain people who enter our lives. We can be anxious about the future and even terrified of what might happen to us and our dear ones. Feeling guilty and fearful about our sins and failures, we can be afraid of facing the Lord in our prayer at home and in our worship together in church. Our fears may hold us back from letting ourselves go into his arms.

Years ago when I enjoyed circus shows, I sometimes saw a stunt on "the wall of death." Daredevil riders on motorcycles would race around seemingly perpendicular walls. They stayed up there, provided they kept moving a high speed. We knew that if their engines failed or if they slowed down too much, they would come off the wall and crash.

The stunt suggested something about our lives. We can spend much of our time racing around and afraid to slow down, to think quietly, and to pray gently. We fear that switching off our engine will make us fall in a heap. But we won't fall into a void. We will find ourselves caught and held by the arms of the Lord.

Give Jesus half a chance. Why should we be afraid? He is the Lord who can calm all storms and save us from all our fears.

❦

Years ago, I heard some friends recalling a famous pessimist called Brown who had a marvelous nickname. They called him "Uphill Brown." I asked those friends to give me some examples of the pessimistic things Uphill Brown used to say. "Well," they told me, "he claimed, for instance, that Our Lord said: 'Few are called and none are chosen.'"

Uphill Brown was certainly changing what we read in Matthew's Gospel: "Many are called but few are chosen" (22:14). This is a serious warning, but it is not gloomy, pessimistic language.

Jesus is very serious about our being delivered from evil and saved for the incredible joy of God's eternal kingdom. We only have one go at life. And Jesus wants us to take that one go, that one great chance, very seriously. But he is not encouraging us to be hopeless pessimists like old Uphill Brown.

God has given each of us a wonderful invitation to an everlasting banquet, a party that will never end. We're invited to follow Jesus and come home to that great celebration that will last forever.

Yes, we do need to take our life very seriously. But we should also live our life with deep trust and great joy. It's God who has invited us, and it's Jesus who calls us and walks with us. It's Jesus who cares for us on our way to eternal life. He certainly wants us to be both called *and* chosen.

You would not be human if you did not have fears?

11

The Only Son of a Widow

I n Luke 7:11–17, Jesus brings the son of a widow back to life. Immediately before this passage, we read of Jesus healing the servant of a centurion in Capernaum (7:1–10). In that story, Jesus exercised his power on behalf of a person who was seriously ill. In this passage, we see Jesus revealing that saving power on behalf of a young man who was already dead and was about to be buried by his widowed mother. Jesus revealed his authority as Lord of life and death.

The widow who had lost her only son did not ask Jesus to do anything for herself or her dead son. Apparently she did not know Jesus: she made no request, and there is no reference in the passage to any faith she might have shown. For her, it seems that Jesus was simply a stranger who stopped when the funeral procession passed through a gate of the town of Nain. It was Jesus himself who took the initiative.

The widow was in deep sorrow and desperate need—without a husband and now without her only son. Jesus had compassion on this widowed mother and said to her: "Do not weep." His heart went out to her. He came forward, and with a simple command ("Young man, I say to you, rise"), he raised her son from the dead.

When Jesus brought the dead man back to life, the crowd "glorified God and said: 'A great prophet has risen among us; God has visited his people.'" Yes, a great prophet had come among them. But "a great prophet" failed to describe adequately someone who raises the dead. Hence, Luke has the people add: "God has visited his people."

Here the Gospel of Luke echoes the words of old Zechariah, which we repeat in the *Benedictus*: "God has *visited* his people and redeemed them" (Luke 1:68). Or, as the same prayer says a few verses later: "The rising sun will *visit* us from on high, to give light to those who sit in darkness and the shadow of death" (Luke 1:78–79). That was exactly what happened in the miracle at Nain: God visited the widow and her son, who were in darkness and the shadow of death.

We don't know the name of the widow or the name of her son. We know where they lived: in Nain, a town about twenty-five miles southwest of Capernaum. We remember them today, because nearly two thousand years ago the Lord of life and death crossed their path. He visited them when they were in darkness and under the shadow of death. This happened because Jesus "had compassion" on the widowed mother, or—as we might translate the Greek verb more accurately—"his heart went out to her."

The same Jesus also has compassion on us. In our troubles, his heart goes out to us, even when we do not take any initiative to approach him. Like the widowed mother, we may make no request of him; our faith in him may seem dormant. No matter, his heart always goes out to us in our needs and sorrows.

We, too, have our deep needs and desperate sorrows. At times we feel that we are burying our last hopes. But we too will meet the Lord Jesus. His heart constantly goes out to us, especially when we know ourselves to sit in darkness and the shadow of death.

As happened long ago at the gate of a small town in Galilee, Jesus continues to show himself to be the rising sun. He never stops visiting us "from on high." He shines on us, when we feel ourselves to be overwhelmed by thick darkness and the very shadow of death.

We can only follow the people of Nain and glorify God, because in Jesus we experience the Lord of life and death. He visits us in all our needs and sorrows. His power and his love never fail to give light to our lives.

— — — — — — — — — — —

12

Two Women Meet Jesus

The mother-in-law of Simon Peter was seriously ill and in bed when she first met Jesus (Mark 1:29–31). Accompanied by Peter, Andrew, James, and John, Jesus turned up in her home, came to her bedside, took her by the hand and lifted her up. Then, "the fever left her, and she began to serve them."

It is worth dwelling on the phrase "she began to serve them." Her restoration to health was so complete that she could immediately begin to do what loving mothers of families always want to do: show hospitality to the guests. She began at once to wait on Jesus, her sons, and the other guests. Yet the text seems to suggest more than instant hospitality offered to guests.

The Greek verb that means "serve," "wait," and even "provide for" will recur in Mark's account of the passion and death of Jesus. Immediately after Jesus died on the cross, we are told of the presence of Mary Magdalene and other women who "used to follow Jesus and *serve, wait on,* or *provide for* him when he was in Galilee" (Mark 15:40–41). They proved themselves faithful disciples, following Jesus from Galilee to Jerusalem and loyally trying to "serve" him right through to his awful death by crucifixion.

The implications of this verb in Mark's Gospel suggests that something more than mere domestic hospitality was involved when Peter's mother-in-law got up at once from her sick bed and "began to serve" Jesus and his companions. She began to be a follower or disciple of Jesus.

We do not know her name but we remember her two thousand years later because of that day, when she was seriously ill and in bed at home, Jesus visited her and changed her life forever. He not only cured her but also made her a disciple, one of those who followed and provided for him. We know very little about Peter's mother-in-law. But what we do know encapsulates two essential features of Christian discipleship. She was healed by him and served him. How could we sum up better what following Jesus involves?

⤫

Luke tells the story of a sinful woman about whom Jesus said something that he never said about anyone else: "She has shown great love" (Luke 7:36–50). In modern times, or at least since the seventeenth century, the idea has spread that love is a feeling, the passionate feeling or interior *disposition* of an individual. Fortunately, there have also been philosophers and theologians who have maintained and developed the truer notion of love as a *relationship*, a mutual relationship between persons. For such thinkers, love is essentially a two-way street, a mutual relating, a giving and a receiving.

Love proves a key theme in that passage from Luke, and it is a genuinely mutual love that shows itself in giving and receiv-

REFLECTIONS FOR BUSY PEOPLE

ing. That is the kind of love which enfolds the whole story. It is a love that emerges in three steps.

First, the woman who has been a notorious sinner behaves toward Jesus with extravagant love. She bathes his feet with her tears, dries them with her hair, and smears them with precious ointment from an alabaster jar.

Second, Jesus defends her by telling the story of a creditor who has two debtors: one owes him 500 denarii (around $50,000) and the other owes him only 50 denarii (around $5,000). When neither of them could pay the money, the creditor generously and lovingly cancels both debts. Both debtors love him in return. But the debtor who had owed 500 denarii loves the kindly creditor even more.

Finally, Jesus praises the sinful woman: "She has shown great love." Nowhere else in the four Gospels does he ever praise anyone as highly as that. One can understand why. Her extravagant love goes beyond any other loving action toward Jesus recorded by the evangelists.

This passage in Luke presents us with an extraordinary story of mutual love: the woman's prodigal love for Jesus and his generous, forgiving love toward her. Jesus gives her his love by forgiving her sins and boldly speaking up for her. He also receives her love and is glad to receive it.

In his 2006 encyclical *Deus Caritas Est* ("God is Love"), Pope Benedict XVI emphasized that love involves receiving as well as giving. It is a matter of needing love as well as exercising benevolent love. Love entails not only giving to others and doing things for them but also receiving love from them.

Jesus gives something wonderful to the woman. He forgives her sins, and acts toward her with a generous love that defends her in the face of self-righteous critics. But Jesus also receives something from her. He wants her love; he even needs her love.

Jesus is ready to do anything for her and for everyone else whom he loves. He is ready to forgive us, defend us, and even die for us. But he also wants our love; he needs our love. He wants to be loved by us—loved greatly and even extravagantly.

We might think of joining the sinful woman in our prayer: imagining ourselves to be kneeling at the feet of Jesus, weeping tears of joy and gratitude, and even joining her in wiping his feet with our hair and smearing his feet with some costly ointment that we have brought.

It might, of course, be unusual and even privately embarrassing for us to exercise our imagination that way in prayer. But Jesus wants our love and he wants it for our own good. He could only be deeply happy if we were to kneel before him with that woman who long ago showed him such great love.

13

The Call of Matthew

"Jesus saw a man called Matthew sitting at a tax booth, and he said to him, 'Follow me'" (Matt 9:9). Every day crowds of tourists visit the church of St. Louis in Rome to see three masterpieces painted by Caravaggio. You find the three paintings on the left, in a chapel dedicated to St. Matthew. The first painting depicts Matthew sitting at his tax booth in his unsavory work of collecting taxes, and being called by Christ to leave that disreputable occupation and become a disciple. The second work represents Matthew writing his Gospel. The third work portrays the martyrdom of Matthew.

Whenever I go into that church, I find a steady stream of visitors. They head for the chapel of St. Matthew and gaze in awed silence at those works by Caravaggio. After taking in the three masterpieces, most people come away with a sense of their favorite painting.

My own choice is the first painting, which portrays the call of Matthew. On one side, Christ stretches out his arm in a way that recalls Michelangelo's depiction of the creation of Adam in the Sistine Chapel. On the other side, there is Matthew sitting at his desk with light shining on his face. He has seen and recognized the divine Light that has come into the world. Behind the extended arm of Christ there is an open window; its woodwork takes the form of a cross.

In a brilliant way, Caravaggio associates the creation of the world, the creation of us, with the incarnation and the divine Light that has broken into our world, and then with the call of Matthew to follow Christ who will be crucified on the wood of the cross. Thus Caravaggio brings together creation, the incarnation, and the crucifixion.

Matthew himself was blessed in three marvelous ways: he was brought into existence by God; he saw and accepted the divine Light that shone from the face of Christ; he was called to share in a mission to the world that entailed the crucifixion of Christ and his own sharing in the passion of his Master.

Caravaggio's painting of Matthew's call brings together three basic and enormous blessings that shape our lives: We have been created and brought into existence. We have seen the glory of God on the face of Christ. We are called as baptized believers to share in a mission to the whole world, which entails the passion of Christ and our own share in that passion.

Matthew showed his joy and gratitude at the way he had been blessed by inviting Jesus to his home, putting on a big dinner, and beginning at once his own mission by drawing other morally disreputable persons into contact with Jesus. We, too, must show our joy and gratitude at the way we have been wonderfully blessed.

> *Lord Jesus, you have called us into existence.*
> *We praise and thank you.*
> *Lord Jesus, we have seen on your face the glorious light*
>   *of God.*
> *We praise and thank you.*
> *Lord Jesus, you have called us, even though sinners, to be*
> *your disciples and to follow you to the cross and then*
>   *to glory.*
> *We praise and thank you.*

14

The Call of Simon and Jude

Since my father's birthday coincides with the feast day of Sts. Simon and Jude (October 28), I have always had a special interest in them. (Jesus calls them in Luke 6:15–16.) In the list of the twelve apostles called by Jesus, Simon and Jude come in the tenth and eleventh place, respectively. They are right at the end, just before Judas Iscariot.

In its note for the feast of Simon and Jude, a missal that I once checked almost apologized for the fact that we know so little about them. "Nothing is known of Simon except that he was born at Cana and was known as the zealot." As for Jude: "Jude, also known as Thaddaeus, was the apostle who, at the Last Supper, asked the Lord why he showed himself only to his disciples and not to the world" (John 14:22).

In one sense, it's discouraging that we know so little about Simon and Jude—about what they did and said, about where they went in the early years of Christianity, about where they preached, and about how and when they died. These two men would have been totally forgotten in world history, but for one thing.

Jesus called them from the wider group of his disciples to join the "core group" of the Twelve. By calling them, Jesus lifted them out of oblivion. He gave them the unique role of joining his original cohort of Christian leaders. We remember Simon and Jude today, two thousand years later, because of what Jesus did for them and what he made of them.

I draw deep encouragement from their feast day and what it conveys. What we *are* and what we are to *become* depends utterly on Jesus. He rescues our lives from oblivion. It's his relationship with us that makes all the difference.

Whenever I preach to a congregation on the feast of Simon and Jude, I remark: "It would be wonderful if there were one or two people present here this morning, who one day will be canonized as saints. Who knows whether we and they may be blessed in that way? Yet the odds are, that in the missals published in a hundred years' time, our names will be not be found, and that we will not have even a couple of lines after our names.

"Yet it doesn't ultimately matter whether church authorities decide to beatify or canonize us, or what anyone says or writes about us in a missal or in any other book. What finally matters is that Jesus has called each of us and given each one of us our special, personal mission. It is his call that fills our lives and our mission with eternal value, so that we will live forever and never be forgotten."

I cherish Simon, Jude, and other persons who turn up ever so briefly in the Gospels. They suggest so beautifully what Jesus has done and continues to do for all of us.

15

Seeing Jesus

A fter a number of chapters telling the story of Jesus' ministry, Luke remarks that Herod Antipas, the ruler of Galilee and the son of Herod the Great, heard about what Jesus was teaching and doing and wanted "to see him" (Luke 9:9). But Herod had to wait quite a while before that meeting happened.

According to Luke, Herod Antipas eventually saw Jesus only after he was betrayed and arrested. That was when, in Luke's story of the passion, Pontius Pilate sent Jesus to be questioned by Herod (23:6–12). What did "seeing Jesus" do for Herod when it finally happened? Not much, as far as we are told. It led Herod and Pilate to patch up some quarrel and become reconciled to each other. And that was all.

This story about Herod Antipas suggests the question: What *was* it like and what *is* it like "to see Jesus"? During his lifetime and at the time of his passion and death, thousands of people saw him. Some of them just happened to be there when Jesus passed by. Some went looking for him out of curiosity. Herod was suffering from a guilty conscience after he had put John the Baptist to death. What Herod was hearing about Jesus troubled him, and he wanted to see Jesus for himself.

What comes through loud and clear from the story of Herod and others in the Gospel is that there were and are many different ways of "seeing Jesus." People could catch a glimpse of him or gaze right at him, but see him only in a merely external, physical way. Yes, they saw him alright, but they didn't really open their eyes to him and take him in. They saw him, but did not recognize him. They failed to see him in any kind of internal, spiritual way. They failed to see him with the eyes of faith and with the eyes of love.

Nowadays we see so many people, the faces of so many people. Through television we are bombarded with the faces of people. We see them in their thousands. We spend our lives seeing others. But what do we really see in them? *Whom* do we see in them?

Every human being is a brother or sister of Jesus. Every human being shows us the face of Jesus. In Belgium, there is a church near the coast that has a remarkable door on the tabernacle. But you have to get up close to see what is carved on that metal door of the tabernacle. The artist has carved dozens of tiny human faces on the door: faces of younger people and older people, faces of men and faces of women. When you get close to that tabernacle, you are looking not only at the eucharistic presence of Jesus, but also at his presence revealed through the faces of other human beings. By seeing them and recognizing them as the brothers and sisters of Jesus, you are truly seeing him.

Poor old Herod Antipas! He wanted "something precious" when he told others: "I want to see Jesus." We too desire something utterly precious whenever we want to see Jesus. But he is *always* there for the seeing—on the faces of all our brothers and sisters. He is there for the seeing in many other ways, and not least through what the eyes of faith and the eyes of love take in when the sacraments are celebrated.

May we all share something of the grace of so many saintly men and women. They wanted to see Jesus and they did see him. They lived their lives seeing Jesus with the eyes of faith and love. May we all be blessed with that special gift, the eyes of faith and love that constantly see Jesus in everyone and in everything that surrounds us.

16

The Sign of Jonah

The figure of Jonah, a reluctant prophet, links together two scriptural passages—Jonah 3:1–10 and Luke 11:29–32. In the passage from the Old Testament, the preaching of Jonah leads the people of Nineveh to repent instantly. This violent and rapacious city has much to regret and do penance for, but universal repentance comes totally and at once. In the Gospel passage, Jesus reproaches his audience for failing to repent when offered "the sign of Jonah," the preaching and presence of Jesus himself.

In terms of lost opportunities, a strong contrast is drawn between the people of Nineveh and the generation of Jesus' contemporaries. The Ninevites are offered only a small window of time for repentance: "Only forty days more and Nineveh will be destroyed." In addition, God sends them an odd, almost comic, figure in the prophet Jonah. Jonah has tried to run away and keep the greatest possible distance between himself and Nineveh. He does not want to sell the divine message to this wicked people. In any case, his warning is extremely terse and sounds like a telegram from on high: "Only forty days more and Nineveh will be destroyed." Jonah is simply not in the class of Ezekiel, Isaiah, and Jeremiah, whose warnings from God were communicated with passion and brilliance and at length. Yet the king and people of Nineveh hear the word of God when this odd stranger comes among them with his laconic warning of doom. They make excellent use of the little that is offered to them and commit themselves at once to a program of prayer and penance. The king, his people, and even their livestock respond by collectively and generously repenting of their evil ways. Seeing this massive act of repentance, God "relented" and did not inflict on the city "the disaster which he had threatened."

In the passage from Luke's Gospel, Jesus rebukes his audience for not responding to the much richer grace they have been offered. In what must be the most remarkable understatement in the entire New Testament, Jesus refers to himself by saying: "There is something greater than Jonah here." For good measure, he throws in as well the example of the Queen of Sheba who had to come "from the ends of the earth to hear the wisdom of Solomon." Separated by a great distance, she came, nevertheless, to hear and profit from the wisdom of King Solomon. Jesus' second example prompts him to make a second remarkable understatement by referring to himself: "There is something greater than Solomon here."

Many of those who hear Jesus' words and see his powerful deeds fail to take advantage of the unique grace they are being offered. They don't have to come from a great distance, like the

Queen of Sheba. Jesus is in their neighborhood and even right there in front of them. They can easily hear and accept the full scope of his abundant preaching, and are not confronted merely with a laconic warning from a disgruntled prophet who turns up unexpectedly. In any case, Jesus is immeasurably greater than any Jonah or Solomon. And yet many in his audience do not "read the sign" that faces them and then open themselves to Jesus. They disappoint him by not repenting and committing themselves to the unique good news that is Jesus and his message.

Our scripture passages about the sign of Jonah converge and lead us to two uncomfortable conclusions. First, those who have few spiritual opportunities sometimes, or even often, make the most of them, whereas those who have been richly privileged can fail to take advantage of what they have been offered. These two texts can suggest the daunting exercise of listing the spiritual privileges and chances with which we have been blessed and then asking ourselves these questions: What have I done with all these opportunities and graces? What am I doing with them? What ought I do with them?

Second, Jonah comes across as a strange figure, an unusual prophet who has to learn so much about the unlimited nature of God's mercy that reaches out to embrace even ruthless sinners, such as the hated Ninevites. Jonah reminds us that God can use surprising signs and unexpected persons to bring us truth and salvation.

Jesus himself, *the* sign of Jonah in person, was also surprising and unexpected. Before they met, Nathanael heard about Jesus being from Nazareth and retorted with astonishment: "Can anything good come out of Nazareth?" (John 1:46). At one point even the family of Jesus seemed concerned about his sanity (Mark 3:21). And some of his listeners were scandalized at the way Jesus ate and drank with public sinners (Luke 7:34).

It is at our peril that we ignore all that made Jesus strange, unexpected, and even scandalous to people of his generation.

May we all be ready to recognize that the surprising, strange, and even shocking persons in our lives may have a message for us from God. After all, there was much that was unexpected about the Son of God himself. He came to surprise us with his grace and shock us with the vehemence of his love for us.

And may we follow in the steps of Nathanael. His first reaction was negative, but Philip did not argue with him. Philip simply asked him to come and experience for himself the man from Nazareth: "Come and see." In other words, "Don't keep your distance and stick with your prejudices. Come to Jesus and really see him for yourself." When Nathanael meets Jesus, they exchange only a few words before Nathanael blurts out his confession: "You are the Son of God! You are the King of Israel" (John 1:49). It is an extraordinary and extraordinarily quick turnaround in Nathanael's life. He makes the richest and deepest confession that comes from any of those pictured in the first chapter of John's Gospel as finding faith in Jesus (Andrew, Simon Peter, Philip, and, finally, Nathanael). Someone from a most unexpected place turns out to be the One to whom Nathanael can now give his total allegiance and true adoration.

By also associating the sign of Jonah with Jesus being rescued from the tomb through his resurrection from the dead, Matthew leads us to the third part of this book and the questions: How did Jesus face his suffering destiny? What did he do in his passion, death, and resurrection?

Part Three

Jesus in His Death and Resurrection

1

Facing the Future

When we reflect on how Jesus might have thought and felt, especially as his passion loomed, we deal with a question at the extreme limit. After all, we are attempting to explore the human mind and human feelings exercised and experienced by the incarnate Son of God.

We need here the sensitivity of a novelist, the faith of a believer, and, perhaps most of all, the prudence of a biblical historian. We are dealing with the consciousness and feelings of someone who lived his earthly life two thousand years ago. We do know a good deal about Jesus from our four Gospels. But they tend very much to report and interpret the visible, public record. For the most part, the Gospels do not say anything directly about the inner life of Jesus. He didn't leave us any diaries or letters that would have enlightened us enormously about his thoughts and feelings.

And yet, even if we behave prudently and respect the cautionary remarks that come from valuable biblical historians, we do have our questions. We can't help asking how people feel, what they know, and what they plan to do. With due caution, as well as with sensitivity and faith, we can raise such questions about the inner life of Jesus, above all the extent and nature of his human knowledge when his suffering and death drew near.

All of this makes what Jesus said about the limits of his knowledge concerning the timing of the end not only intriguing but also valuable for us: "About that day or hour no one knows, neither the angels in heaven nor the Son [on earth], but only the Father" (Mark 13:32). Right from the first century, some Christians found this admission a bit embarrassing. How could he admit that he didn't know the answer to such an important question as the timing of the end of history? And yet Mark recalls this frank admission on the part of Jesus.

The future, even the future completion of the divine work that Jesus is doing on earth, remains hidden to him—at least in his human mind. He is the central protagonist of the great divine project of our redemption, but its future fulfillment remains shrouded in mystery, even for him.

To be sure, Jesus differs from us not merely in degree but also in kind. He knows his own unique identity as God the Son. That identity sets him quite "apart" from us. But he is like us, in that he, too, has to leave something of the future in the hands of his Father. He walks toward that future with total love and obedience. Yet, it is a future that remains at least somewhat mysterious even to him.

It can be deeply comforting to realize that, along with ourselves, Jesus himself was somewhat in the dark about the future. He, too, had to entrust it to the loving care and concern of his Father.

The Gospels, or at least the Gospel According to Mark, rarely let us catch anything of Jesus' inner life and feelings. This reticence makes the occasional glimpses even more valuable. The verse I have quoted from Mark provides one of those rare glimpses. Jesus walked toward a future that was still partly unknown to him. We are called to walk with him toward our own future, a future that is still mysterious. But it is a future that we, too, can safely leave in the hands of our all-powerful and all-loving God.

-- -- -- -- -- -- -- --

2

Eating and Drinking

The respectable people of Jesus' day actively separated themselves from those who lived outside the bounds of decent society. They did not want to be contaminated by them. Jesus, however, did just the opposite. He sought the company of the unsavory members of his society. He reached out to them, shared meals with them, and did his best to meet their needs.

Such a preference on the part of Jesus prompted ugly criticism: "Look, a glutton and a drunkard, a friend of tax collectors and sinners" (Luke 7:34). It was a nasty sneer. But for all that, the sneer expressed something profoundly true about Jesus and his habits. For him, eating and drinking with others provided a way of entering into communion with all kinds of people, especially those with serious spiritual needs. They found him to be a wonderful friend to be with, someone who never turned anyone away, and a person who changed their lives—often by simply eating and drinking with them.

Both then and now, eating and drinking with others are very normal activities. Jesus, however, did normal things in his own unique way. He used such normal things as meals together as a means to heal people and create deep communion and lasting friendship. Those meals reached their climax on the night before he died, when he used a meal to institute the Eucharist.

At the Last Supper, Jesus took some bread and said: "This is my body that is for you." He then took a cup of wine and said: "This cup is the new covenant in my blood."

When instituting the Eucharist, Jesus used something to be eaten and something to be drunk: some bread and some wine. His choice of these elements was affected, of course, by the setting of the Last Supper: the celebration of the Jewish Passover. Tradition played its part in the choice Jesus made.

But we can step back from the Passover setting and ask the broader question: What did bread and wine mean at his time and in his culture and, for that matter, in many other cultures? Bread, the staff of life, obviously stood for survival. You needed bread on your table, if you were to survive and go on living and working. And wine? Wine stood for celebration. Every now and then there was a feast, and people could drink some wine in celebration. Both then and now, we all need to survive and to celebrate.

There's no point in mere survival, merely getting through life in a tight-lipped kind of way, with all the joy of celebration gone out of our existence. But there's no point either in empty celebration, if we no longer have the strength to live as we ought to live. We need to celebrate with strength and survive with joy.

In the Eucharist, the bread and wine become the Body and Blood of the crucified and risen Jesus. It's *that* Body and Blood that constitute the real bread of life and the true wine of celebration.

Let us pray for ourselves, and for all our brothers and sisters in the church, that the Eucharist will give us, day by day, the grace to celebrate with strength and survive with joy. Let us praise Jesus, the special friend of tax collectors and sinners. He used and uses a holy eating and drinking as *the* way for transforming our lives and entering into communion and friendship with us now and forever.

His critics sneered at Jesus as if he were a glutton and a drunkard or someone who ate and drank to excess. Without realizing it, these querulous critics pointed to something profoundly true about Jesus. He did go to excess—in his love for us sinners and not least through giving us the Eucharist, where we eat his Body and drink his Blood. The extravagant, excessive love of Jesus created that holy eating and drinking, which allows us to celebrate with strength and survive with joy.

3

Arranging for the Son to Be Killed

Sometimes described in the United Kingdom as a "national treasure," John Humphrys has reported for the BBC for over forty years and been a frontline presenter of news programs for both radio and television. His book *In God We Doubt* takes readers along the road he traveled from a Christian upbringing to agnostic doubt about the existence of God. With charming honesty, he sets out not only his respect for religious faith but also the reasons for his own agnostic position.

One stumbling block for Humphrys comes from what he has heard some Christians say when they explain the death of Jesus: "God arranged to have his own Son brutally killed because that would somehow atone for all our sins. But being killed was a good thing, because after Jesus died, he rose from the dead and ascended into heaven." Humphrys admits that this is a parody. But his parody is uncomfortably close to the account that believers at times offer of atonement.

When they reflect on the passion and death of Jesus, many Christians feel obliged to ask: "In God's plan, did Jesus have to suffer and die?" They recall that reproach to the two disciples on the road to Emmaus: "Was it not *necessary* that Christ should suffer these things and enter into his glory?" (Luke 24:20). When Jesus predicted his passion, he spoke in similar tones: "The Son of Man *must* suffer many things…and be killed and after three days rise again" (Mark 8:31). St. Paul cited an early Christian Creed that strikes the same note of necessity: "Christ died for our sins in accordance with the scriptures" (1 Cor 15:3). Those early Christians who knew their scriptures could see that the crucifixion *had* to be. The first Christians discerned in the event of Calvary much more than a cruel killing that put a violent end to the life of Jesus. They acknowledged that in the divine plan for human salvation it needed to be so.

But does that mean believing that God *directly* "arranged to have his own Son brutally killed"? Was that the only way to atone for all the sins of human beings? What sense can we detect in the "must" of Jesus' death by public execution?

Some medieval theologians mitigated any "absolute necessity" of the crucifixion by arguing that, at least in theory, Jesus could have saved the human race by undergoing any act of suffering, even by shedding one drop of his blood. Nowadays many thinkers want to leave behind such speculations. On what grounds can we imagine or even dictate alternative scenarios for God's plan to redeem humanity? It is more convincing to take up the "must" of Calvary on the *historical* level, and appreciate how it was unavoidable in *human* terms.

At all times in the history of the human race, prophets have been persecuted for refusing to be moderate and accommodating and for faithfully transmitting some message from God. Jesus' fidelity to his mission for God's kingdom inevitably brought him into conflict with the powerful political and religious people of his day. In such a conflict he was—humanly speaking—bound to lose. Even a moderately astute analyst of political-religious affairs in first-century Palestine would have reached that conclusion. Human power and malice made Jesus' suffering and death inevitable.

Back in the fourth century BC, Plato had suggested in the introduction to Book II of his *Republic* the kind of fate that a perfectly just man could expect in our violent and unjust world: "The just man, then, as we have pictured him, will be scourged, tortured, and imprisoned, his eyes will be put out, and after enduring every humiliation he will be crucified."

Christians found this to be a remarkable pagan prophecy of what happened to Jesus himself. Prophecy or not, Plato's words have been fulfilled with depressing frequency. Society continues to make uncompromisingly good individuals suffer both for what they are and for what they try to do. In the case of Jesus, the wonder is not so much that he was struck down so quickly but that he lasted as long as he did.

Besides human malice and violence, something else on the historical scene fed into the "must" of Jesus' passion: his own unswerving fidelity to his God-given mission and the service of others. He was driven by one desire only—that of advancing the kingdom of God. In these terms, Calvary became the inevitable consequence of a commitment that Jesus refused to abandon even at the cost of his life.

Simply by itself, his being savagely killed, along with his experiencing the terrible pain and appalling humiliation involved in crucifixion, was not a "good thing." But it was a uniquely moving sign of love, both of Jesus' self-sacrificing love for us and of the infinite love that allowed our loving God to accept the extreme consequences of sending his only Son to take on our created condition and become our friend and brother. Calvary came about through a mysterious convergence of human malice and divine love.

God is no celestial sadist who delights in pain, nor a hard judge who demands the suffering and cruel death of his Son as the price of redemption. His Son entered a world pervaded by immense suffering, violence, and hatred. Both Christ and his heavenly Father willed the crucifixion indirectly — by accepting it.

Ordinary logic alone can never come even close to explaining and justifying what happened to Christ in his passion and death. Love, above all divine love, has its own logic, which sustains all that it has created and longs to be reconciled with alienated sinners. God cannot *not* love, and love always puts those who love at risk.

Generous, self-sacrificing, and unconditional love—which is what we find exemplified supremely in Christ—makes itself vulnerable and always risks being exploited, rejected, and murderously crushed. Loving service to those in need can turn people into targets. The last few decades have witnessed numerous Good Samaritans in Africa, Asia, and Latin America paying with their lives because they stopped for wounded travelers. Few novelists have pictured the vulnerability of love more brilliantly and disturbingly than Graham Greene in his novel *The Human Factor*. The central character, Maurice Castle, describes love as "a total risk," and he pays a high price for his devoted love to his wife and her son.

The cost of love put Jesus at mortal risk and eventually cost him everything. In the midst of pagan selfishness, cruelty, and despair, his self-sacrificing love shone from the cross. In various languages, a wise choice calls Jesus' suffering and death his "passion," a term that combines intense love with the mortal suffering it brought our divine lover.

Medieval Christians cherished the love that inspired Christ to accept his suffering. They transformed his cry on the cross—"I thirst" (John 19:28)—into a cry of love. A prayer by St. Richard of Chichester captures the best of a tender devotion to Christ on the cross. I hope that John Humphrys might one day go to Chichester and even kneel at the tomb of St. Richard to recite this prayer which he will find there.

> *Thanks be to thee, my Lord Jesus Christ,*
> *for all the benefits which thou hast given me,*
> *for all the pains and insults thou hast borne for me.*
> *O most merciful Redeemer, Friend, and Brother,*
> *may I know thee more clearly,*
> *love thee more dearly*
> *and follow thee more nearly.*

4

Matthew and Mark on the Passion

Essentially the four Gospel writers tell the same story when they report at length the suffering, death, and burial of Jesus. Yet attentive reading of their texts will catch various emphases and insights that are special to them.

Prayerfully reflecting on their passion stories and carefully comparing them can help us appreciate what Jesus went through for us. Let me take two themes from Mark and one from Matthew.

(1) Mark repeatedly uses the verb *to hand over* (in Greek, *paradidomi*) when describing what happened to Jesus. Judas planned to "hand over" Jesus to his enemies (14:10–11). The chief priests bound Jesus, led him away, and "handed him over" to Pontius Pilate, the Roman governor of Judea. In his turn, after having Jesus scourged, Pilate "handed him over" to be crucified. Different people abuse their power by acting against Jesus and keep "handing him over"—eventually to be brutally flogged and then nailed to a cross.

While all this was happening to Jesus, no one stood by or spoke up for him. From the time of his arrest until the moment of his death on the cross, he seemed quite isolated and undefended. He received no visible, human support from anyone. Only a few chapters before he came to the passion narrative, Mark reports the boast that Peter made on behalf of the disciples: "We have left all things and followed you" (10:28). But, when a paramilitary force arrived to arrest Jesus in the Garden of Gethsemane, all the disciples abandoned Jesus and fled in fear. They behaved like cowardly deserters. A mysterious "young man," presumably a disciple of Jesus, symbolized their defection when he left his garment in the hands of the arresting party and fled naked into the night. He left everything to get *away* from Jesus (14:50–52).

As things move breathlessly to the climax on Calvary, Mark's narrative does not include any people who speak up for Jesus. Here he differs from the other Gospel writers. Matthew tells of a painful dream about Jesus that prompted Pilate's wife to send a message to her husband: "Have nothing to do with that innocent man" (Matt 27:19). Luke mentions the women who wept for Jesus on the way to the cross (Luke 23:27) and the criminal who was crucified with Jesus and spoke up for him: "This man has done nothing wrong" (Luke 23:41).

But in Mark's passion story, Jesus is utterly alone and unsupported, from Gethsemane to Calvary. It is only *after* he dies that we learn of the holy women who had been courageously present at the crucifixion (15:40–41) and that we hear the confession of the Roman centurion: "Truly this man was the Son of God" (15:39). But it is in terrible loneliness, according to Mark's narrative, that Jesus goes through his passion right up to death.

(2) Among the challenging themes that color Matthew's passion narrative, one should recall how different characters try to shake off their responsibility for what is happening to Jesus. Judas brings the thirty pieces of silver back and tries to return the money to the chief priests and elders. "I have sinned," he says. "I have brought an innocent man to his death." But they won't accept the money from him. So he throws it down on the ground and goes off to hang himself (Matt 27:3–5).

Then the chief priests, in a way, try to shake off their responsibility. They take the money, but do not put it into the temple fund. They use it to buy a field to serve as a burial place for foreigners (Matt 27:6–10). Pilate also tries to deny his responsibility for Jesus' fate by taking water and washing his hands in full view of the crowd (Matt 27:24).

When we see leading people in Matthew's story trying to disown their responsibility, we can only ask: Who then was responsible for the death of Jesus? One can hardly read the story without feeling a haunting sense of common responsibility, responsibility that even *we* share with Judas, the chief priests, and Pilate. These figures represent all of humanity: Judas represents the followers of Jesus, the chief priests represent the Jews, and Pilate represents the rest of humanity. Two individuals and a small group stand in for all of us. The sins of treachery and expediency that lead them to collaborate in sending Jesus to his death belong to us all.

Gazing at Jesus on the cross, we can only say: "I played my part in that. Lord, have mercy on me and remember me when you come into your kingdom."

---·---·---·---·---

5

The Dead Jesus

Many tourists and pilgrims to Rome carry away at least one vivid memory of their visit to St. Peter's Basilica: the *Pietà* by Michelangelo. The passion and death of Jesus come home to them when they contemplate his crucified body lying limp in his mother's arms.

The whole human story of Jesus is written in his lifeless body. It allows us to look back and recall what he did for human beings during his lifetime and what they did to him. We can focus in turn on his eyes, his mouth, his ears, his hands, and his feet.

His *eyes* are closed: those eyes which looked across crowds of people who were like sheep that were lost and anxious to find a true shepherd. His eyes smiled at children, and blazed with anger at those who put their version of the law above the real needs of suffering people. His eyes filled with tears over the death of a friend, gazed with compassion at the sick, and looked steadily at his disciples when he asked: "Who do you say that I am?"

At the end, what did Jesus see in his passion? Judas coming to betray him with a kiss, the other disciples running away through the olive trees in Gethsemane, and Peter breaking down in grief at denying his Master. What did the eyes of Jesus see when he made his way to Calvary and hung on the cross? And then those eyes finally closed, not in sleep but in death.

His *mouth* is shut and silent: that mouth which announced "Blessed are they that mourn," told the story of the prodigal son leaving and then returning to his family, invited people to "come, follow me," and then declared on the night before he died: "This is my body. This is my blood poured out for you." At the end, that mouth, which had said so many golden, truthful, and loving words, was finally silent in death.

His *ears* are deaf: those ears that listened to the cry of the blind beggar ("Jesus, Son of David, have mercy on me"), took in Peter's confession ("You are the Messiah"), and responded to Levi's invitation to be the guest of honor at a great party. Think, too, of what Jesus' ears had to hear at the end: Peter's boast ("Even if others fall away, I will not"), the cry for his death ("Crucify him, crucify him"), and the mockery on the cross ("Save yourself and come down from the cross"). And then, in death, his ears could listen no more to any of the words or sounds of our world.

When Michelangelo and other great artists portrayed Jesus dead in his mother's arms, they made much of his hands and his feet. His *hands* are torn and lifeless: those hands that touched a leper, healed blind eyes, blessed sinners, lifted up the sick, broke the bread, and shared the cup. His hands had lifted up the feet of the disciples and washed them. Those hands were finally stretched out on a cross, and in death hung down torn and lifeless in the arms of Joseph of Arimathea and Mary.

His *feet* hang motionless: those feet which stepped into the river Jordan for his baptism, walked the roads of Galilee, took him to Levi's party, and carried him on the way to the cross going up to Jerusalem. They were then pinned helplessly to the cross.

His *heart* has stopped and his *brain* is dead: that brain which shaped his golden words and that heart which beat with great compassion for the bewildered crowds of people and for the widowed mother following her son's death.

Yes, the *Pietà* of Michelangelo offers us a most moving way of remembering the suffering and death of Jesus and the love which led him to his end and left him dead in his mother's arms.

Please take time to think about Christ's dead body. The whole story of his life and love are written on that body, now held limp and lifeless in the arms of Mary.

- - - - - - - - -

6

Something New in the World — Easter!

S ome years ago, when ending a course on the resurrection, the students joined me for a eucharistic liturgy. At the presentation of the gifts, each brought to the altar a gift symbolizing the Easter mystery. At the end of the line came two tall students, Mimi and Matthew. When they walked up with nothing in their hands, I wondered whether they would produce something from their pockets. Mimi stopped and then stepped out of her shoes. "They are brand-new shoes," she told us. "The resurrection lets us walk in new ways." Matthew turned toward the congregation and said: "As my Easter gift, I have a new song to teach you."

Mimi and Matthew were right. The resurrection does put new shoes on our feet and a new song in our mouth. By rising from the dead, Jesus empowers us to walk in new ways and to sing his new song of joy, "Alleluia!"

We often hear and sometimes use the term *paschal mystery*. Here *mystery* is no murder mystery to be solved by some Sherlock Holmes. It means the wonderful, life-giving reality of our redemption, which divine love brought about through the suffering, death, and resurrection of Jesus. By calling this reality paschal, we recall the deliverance from the bondage of Egypt celebrated in the Jewish feast of Passover. In other words, the paschal mystery is the marvelous truth of our being saved from sin and evil, and our being set free to live new lives.

Through the paschal mystery of Good Friday and Easter Sunday, God has truly "made all things new" (Rev 21:5). To be sure, it is tempting to join the classical pessimist of the Bible, Qoheleth, who assured us that "there is nothing new under the sun" (Eccl 1:9). At times, our lives can look so gray, dull, and unchangeable that we feel that "there can *be* nothing new for us under *our* sun." The "reasonable" thing is to join the three holy women who remembered the huge stone locking Jesus' body away in darkness and who anxiously asked themselves: "Who will roll away the stone for us from the door of the tomb?" (Mark 16:3). Any of us can feel so dead and locked up that any exit seems impossible. Who will solve *my* great difficulty and roll away *my* persistent problem?

The Easter news, however, is that Jesus is risen. God has done the impossible and brought the dead Jesus to new, transformed life. We, too, are set free from bondage to sing our new songs and live in new ways.

That is the message conveyed by many symbols in the Easter Vigil liturgy. A new Easter candle is blessed, lit, and carried solemnly into the sanctuary. We bring fresh cloths and new flowers to the altar. The celebrant blesses fresh water for baptism and consecrates new hosts. Christ is risen from the dead, and all things are made new.

We learn to love through being loved by Christ and letting ourselves be loved by him. Jesus opens our hearts and enables us to give him and others the only thing he wants: our love. Yet sooner or later, the questions force themselves on us: "Is death the end of everything we have experienced through the love we receive and give? Do we love each other only to have our hearts broken at the end?"

What the resurrection of Christ promises us is that the world to which we go is no gray haunt of ghosts. It will be a totally satisfying experience in which we will know the glorious Christ and all our dear ones, and will be known by them. We have the Lord's promise: "If I go and prepare a place for you, I shall come again and take you to myself, so that where I am you also may be" (John 14:3).

Easter is the wonderful morning after the terrible night of the cross. On Good Friday, evil did its worst. It seemed the end of all things. Christ, the most loving and lovable person we ever had on earth, died a brutal death as a criminal. His end killed the hopes of his friends. With his burial, what was left?

But death could not hold him. He returned, wonderfully transformed, from beyond the grave. He showed himself gloriously alive to those who had known him and seen him die. He met them in the old, familiar places and talked with them about the work he wanted them to do. He taught them to trust him and believe in his presence, even when they would no longer see him visibly.

We, too, enjoy the promise: "I will be with you all days, even to the end of the world" (Matt 28: 20). Easter is the wonderful morning that will never end. The paschal mystery has everything to do with our lives, here and hereafter.

7

"Who will roll away the stone?"

From start to finish, Mark's Gospel features a number of women: Peter's mother-in-law who is sick (1:29–31), the Syrophoenician woman whose daughter is possessed by a evil spirit (7:24–30), the woman who anoints Jesus in the home of Simon the leper (14:3–9), and the three women who visit the tomb of Jesus at the end (16:1–8). It is only very rarely in Mark's story that these and other women speak. The Syrophoenician woman does, and becomes the only person in the any of the four Gospels who wins an argument with Jesus.

But it is only twice in the Gospel of Mark that we find *women talking together*. The first occasion turns up when two women, Herodias and her daughter Salome, plot the death of John the Baptist (6:14–29). Angered that John has challenged her sinful union with her brother-in-law, Herodias tells Salome to ask King Herod for "the head of John the Baptist on a platter." The other occasion comes when Mary Magdalene, Mary the mother of James, and obviously another Salome buy spices to anoint the corpse of Jesus. Then on their way to his tomb they anxiously ask each other: "Who will roll away the stone from the door of the tomb?" (16:3).

Herodias and her daughter are driven by hatred to instigate a sordid killing of a great prophet, who is the immediate fore-runner of Jesus. They have the power and influence to bring about John's death. The murder seemingly takes place late at night, after Salome has danced during the birthday party of King Herod and pleased him with her presumably erotic routine.

Mary Magdalene and her two companions are driven by love and a desire to perform a last act of service for their crucified Master. Darkness enveloped the earth at the time of the crucifixion (15:33), but the sun has just risen when the three women go to the tomb (16:2). The light is streaming into the sky when something they never imagined is about to be revealed to them. God has been at work to bring about what is humanly impossible by opening a tomb and raising the dead Jesus to gloriously transformed life. With the resurrection, God has definitively overcome darkness and death. The women are walking into a new day that will never end.

Whether Mark consciously intended this or not, we find a striking contrast between the two occasions when women speak to another in his Gospel. On the first occasion, hatred prompts a sordid deed of murder during the darkness of the night. Herodias and her daughter use the human power of a king to bring about an ugly killing.

On the second occasion, love inspires a visit to a tomb as dawn breaks and a wonderful new day begins. The three women want to do something beautiful for Jesus. He has been dreadfully victimized and destroyed by the unjust use of human power. Now God surprises the women with the radiant new life of the resurrection that the power of divine love has brought about.

To be sure, Herodias and Salome are an unlikely pair to set in contrast with Mary Magdalene and her two companions. But the sheer ugliness of their murderous deed may help us to appreciate even more the beautiful love of the three women. They visit the tomb of Jesus and are astonished to find how the love of God has dramatically reversed a situation of death and injustice. There is much to value about the three women who ask each other, "Who will roll away the stone?"—and then find the tomb of Jesus open and empty.

- - - - - - - - - -

8

Seeing Where We Buried Them

On the first Easter Sunday morning, when the three holy women enter the tomb of Jesus, they are told: "He has been raised. He is not here. See the place where they buried him" (Mark 16:6). Yes, see the place where they buried him.

Our lives are full of people and places that are dead and buried. Many of us have already lost one of our parents. All of us have dead friends to remember and mourn. At times we go to see where we buried them. There are all those places in New York, Philadelphia, Los Angeles, Phoenix, London, Dublin, as well as other cities, states, and countries where we have laid our dead to rest.

There are also the people and places that in other ways have gone out of our lives, never to be seen again. We may remember the boys and girls who were our companions at high school or college, the neighbors on the street where we once lived before shifting to another suburb or another city.

We can recall, too, those people who for a few years shared with us our journey through life—in the same workplace, in the same parish, or in the same business building. How few of them have stayed in our lives! Memory brings back the places, but the people are gone, many of them forever.

Yes, we can see the places where we laid our dead and buried our past. There are so many faces and voices that have gone out of our lives.

But what we draw from the resurrection of Jesus is the sure hope that none of those faces are gone forever, the certain trust that none of those voices will be really silent forever. In Christ, the dead and buried will rise again. Of all those faces and voices that we knew and loved, none will be finally lost to us in the silence of the grave.

Christ died and rose, in order to gather into one the children of God who have been scattered (John 11:52). Some of God's children who walked with us, perhaps for many years, have already been scattered and lost in death. Other children of God, who were with us for a time, have slipped away as we changed places. There are all those silent tombs and empty places in our lives. But those tombs and places that have seemingly taken away and scattered the children of God do not have the final say.

Like the holy women in the tomb on the first Easter Sunday, we hear the words: "See the place where they buried him." But we also remember the words: "He has been raised; he is not here."

And we remember as well the promise Jesus made to gather into one the children of God who have been scattered. People whom we know and cherish constantly go out of our lives. They are taken away by death in all its many forms. We lose people and bury our dead.

But Jesus will come again and take us to himself, so that where he is, we also may be (John 14:3). He gives us the hope that no voice and no face will be gone from us forever in death.

We lay our dead to rest, but, thanks to Jesus, none of them are finally gone out of our lives.

9

Seeing with Our Heart

Many people tell us that love is blind. They are convinced that lovers can't see things properly and are sure to miss the truth. I don't agree with these pessimists. Frankly, I think we see best with our hearts. Those who love are quick to catch the truth.

My favorite example of someone who sees with his heart comes from St. John's Gospel. Do you remember that mysterious character who begins to appear in John's Gospel at the Last Supper, the beloved disciple who is so close to Jesus? He was there at the side of Jesus when they all ate together. When Jesus was arrested, he did not run away but followed the Lord into the courtyard of the high priest. A chapter later in John, it is no surprise to find the beloved disciple standing at the foot of the cross with Jesus' mother and with Mary Magdalene.

On Easter Sunday, after Mary Magdalene reported that she found Jesus' tomb to be open and empty, the beloved disciple ran to the tomb. When he entered the tomb, "he sees and believes" (John 20:8). He became the first person in John's Gospel to believe that Jesus is risen from the dead. He saw the empty tomb and the burial garments left there, and he leaped straight to faith. He was the only person in any of the four

Gospels whose Easter faith did not have to be triggered by see-ing the risen Jesus himself.

What made the beloved disciple so ready to believe? It was his special love that lets him "read" an ambiguous sign like the empty tomb. It was love that made him jump straight to the truth. A special bond of friendship had grown between him and Jesus. That loving friendship made him share the suffering and death of the Lord. He did not run away like the other male disciples, but took his place at the foot of the cross. He loved Jesus and would care for Jesus' mother. And then, on the first Easter morning, it was his love that led him straight to his new, Easter faith.

Love is not blind. We see with our hearts. It was his heart that allowed the beloved disciple to see at once the truth of Jesus' resurrection from the dead. This disciple loved Jesus, saw his Master with the eyes of love, and was predisposed to know and believe instinctively what had happened: Jesus is risen.

Each of us needs that kind of love, the love that will keep us close to Our Lord at all times. Love can keep us there with Jesus in good times and in bad times, in joy and in sorrow, at happy meals and during grim crucifixions.

When love keeps us near Jesus, we will have eyes to see him in his glorious resurrection. Love will let us see his risen power in our lives.

Without love, we are just voices whispering in the dark. But with love, the darkness goes away, our eyes see, faith comes, and faith remains strong. With love, we can see and believe, and keep on believing in Jesus, our risen Lord.

Don't be afraid to see with your heart.

10

The Easter Diary of Christopher Hope Mitchell

Verity and Alan Mitchell would not accept an abortion, even though doctors had discovered that their unborn son suffered from Edwards syndrome. This always-fatal genetic disease kills most babies in utero; those who survive to delivery die usually within the first month. When the boy was born in November 1996, the Mitchells named him Christopher Hope, "Christ-bearer of Hope." Before he died a few months later, the Mitchells sent their friends two bulletins in his name. Here is the second of those bulletins:

* * *

It seems an awfully long time since I sent you my first letter and, although I have seen some of my friends regularly, there are some people I haven't met yet. So I thought all of you might like to know how I have been getting on.

I still weigh only four pounds fourteen ounces, which is half a pound less than my birth weight, but curiously enough I have managed to grow one inch longer. I have a very slow heart rate and rather irregular breathing. I use up all my strength just to stay as I am, so I don't have any spare energy for growing.

When I was four months old, I had a checkup at the hospital, and all the doctors seemed very pleased with me. They said I was extra special, because no one thought that I would survive as long as this. The consultant asked if my Mummy would bring me in again another day, so that the hospital photographer could take some pictures of me to put in the big fat file that has my name on the outside. I must say I thought this seemed very odd, since Mummy and Daddy already have hundreds of photos of me. Two people have even taken videos of me. I like these, because if you listen carefully, you can hear me squeaking in the background.

No one seems to know how much longer I will live, but I've successfully passed various landmarks over the last few months. The first was just to be born alive. I am so grateful that Mummy was prepared to have a caesarean operation, because otherwise I might well have died during labor. The next stage was the two weeks I spent in the Special Care Baby Unit in the hospital, before I was allowed to come home. That was a really exciting day, especially as it was snowing.

When the rector at All Souls heard that I might not live for very long, he said that I could have a special baptism as part of an evening service. The church was absolutely packed. When Mum and Dad explained why I was so special, lots of people had to reach for their hankies. I am now the smallest member of the church family. There was someone in the congregation from Premier, the new radio station in London, and he asked if they could do a feature about me during the following week. Lots more people were able to hear my story.

Christmas was the next landmark, then Mother's Day (I picked some daffodils from the garden with Daddy's help and brought Mummy breakfast in bed). Now here we are almost at Easter. I am about to go on holiday to Cornwall and visit my grandaunt, and just the other day I heard Mummy saying that she might have to get me a passport for my summer holiday.

I have made lots and lots of friends, although it is a bit odd when I meet other babies that are the same age as me, since they usually seem to be twice as big as I am.

One of the interesting things I have done is to visit our local hospice, St. Christopher's (nice name), where they have a special service when someone puts their hands on my head and says a prayer for me. Mummy and I then go and visit some of the patients who are dying. Often they like to hold me, and it seems to help them know that it is not just elderly people who need terminal care.

Mum and Dad say that having me around has helped them deepen a lot of their friendships. People seem to open up much more about their own pains and sorrows, and we have heard some very sad stories about multiple miscarriages or children who have died young. Some people use big words to talk about the theology of suffering, but I think perhaps they have missed the point. I'm not really suffering pain at all. I get sticky eyes and a sore bottom occasionally, but that is really no different from other babies. It's just that, because of an extra chromosome, I am not going to live for very long.

Nowadays, many fetal abnormalities can be spotted early in the pregnancy, and the result is that most babies like me, or even those who have just a small handicap, are terminated before birth. I often hear Mum and Dad say that they are so glad that they didn't deny me the chance to live. I don't ask for very much, just Mummy's milk, warmth, and lots of cuddles. Some doctors say that my condition is "incompatible with life" or that I cannot have "a meaningful life." Well, it may not be compatible with long-term survival, but perhaps I am supposed to have a life span of only a certain length—and that length is short. And who is to say what is meaningful? I don't suppose I am going to achieve very much in one sense, but that doesn't mean that I have nothing to offer. I'm the person that I am, and I'm sure my life does have a purpose. I must have been cuddled by well over a hundred people by now, and I suspect many of them will remember me long after I have gone.

If it is true that we are made in the image of God, then I perhaps reflect a Good Friday portrait of God, the broken body of Christ on the cross. Of course, the wonderful news of Easter Day for me is that Jesus came back from the grave in a new resurrection body. In eternal life I will not be deformed, weak, or helpless any more. I will be a new creation.

Lots of love,
Christopher

‒ ∙ ‒ ∙ ‒ ∙ ‒ ∙ ‒ ∙ ‒

11

A Shadowy Witness to the Resurrection

Chapter 1 of the Acts of the Apostles records how a certain Matthias was chosen to fill the vacancy left in the "college" of the twelve apostles by the defection and death of Judas Iscariot. We are told very little about Matthias—nothing about his birthplace, his age, his family, his education, or his personal characteristics. All we learn about him is that he had joined Jesus during the ministry and, we presume, could personally witness to the resurrection because he had probably been present on at least one occasion when the risen Jesus appeared to his followers (Acts 1:21–26). Matthias would be there on the day of Pentecost when the Holy Spirit descended with power. One can also suppose that he belonged to the group of the apostles in Jerusalem to which the early chapters of Acts refer (e.g., 2:37, 42), especially when the group is called the Twelve (6:2). That is all we learn about Matthias—in fact, from only one book of the New Testament, the Acts of the Apostles. Otherwise, he remains an elusive, shadowy figure.

Some ancient traditions alleged that Matthias preached in Ethiopia. In Alexandria, Basilides, a second-century teacher of esoteric wisdom on the fringes of mainstream Christianity, exploited the obscure status of Matthias by making him the source of strange, new doctrines, which were based on "secret sayings" of Jesus transmitted orally from the apostle Matthias himself—or so Basilides said.

But in terms of actually known history, Matthias remains elusive and obscure, even liturgically: Catholics in the West celebrate his feast on May 14; Anglicans remember him on February 24; and the Greek Orthodox have made August 9 his feast day. Both historically and liturgically, Matthias seems shadowy and almost without a fixed tenure.

What lifts him out of oblivion and gives him his lasting place is Jesus' friendship with and love for him. In John's Gospel for Matthias' feast day on May 14, we hear Jesus saying: "As the Father loved me, so have I loved you"; "You are my friends"; "I call you friends" (John 15:9–17). These words describe the heart of Matthias' situation and destiny. Jesus chose him, called him friend, and loved him. That choice, that call, and that love lifted Matthias out of oblivion and made him, in the aftermath of the resurrection and on the eve of Pentecost, one of the twelve apostles. It is only because of the loving initiative of Jesus that, two thousand years later, we recall Matthias, a friend chosen and loved by his Lord.

To each of us also, Jesus addresses those precious words: "I chose you and have called you friend....As the Father loved me, so have I loved you." That choice, that call, and that love lift all of us out of shadowy oblivion and have brought us into fellowship with Jesus. Jesus himself is our tenure, the one who gives us our lasting place in history.

Ultimately, it won't matter whether we go to preach in Ethiopia or whether some latter-day eccentric oddball thinks we are the greatest. It won't matter whether anyone celebrates our passing to the Lord on February 24, May 14, or August 9. Despite that, we are no longer obscure, elusive, shadowy figures. Jesus has loved us and called us his friends.

For Matthias and for each of us, what finally makes all the difference is that Jesus says to us: "As the Father has loved me, so have I loved you."

12

Waiting for Faustus

I n his *Confessions*, St. Augustine wrote about his experiences and beliefs before he became a Christian. For nine years he belonged to a sect called the Manichees. Manichaeism was a religion that started in ancient Persia and that despised the material side of our human existence. According to the Manichees, there is a spark of light within us. That spark needs to be delivered from darkness and from the evil, physical side of our human condition.

After a while, Augustine began to have serious difficulties with the beliefs of the Manichees but he decided to wait for a special Manichaean teacher who was going to come and untangle all the difficulties that Augustine felt. This special teacher,

Faustus, lived out of town. Once Faustus arrived, everything was going to be cleared up. All of Augustine's questions would be answered. His problems would be solved, and life would really begin.

But when Faustus arrived, none of that untangling happened. Intellectually, Faustus was no match for Augustine. He simply could not answer the deep difficulties that Augustine raised about the beliefs of the Manichees. Augustine had been suffering from what might be called the "waiting-for-Faustus" syndrome.

I wonder whether some of us may also sometimes suffer from the same "waiting-for-Faustus" syndrome. One day somebody truly special is going to arrive from Bangalore, from Kyoto, or from San Francisco, and that person is going to tell me what life is really about. One day I will take the course or find the book that is really going to get my spiritual life started for the first time.

If we do suffer from the "waiting-for-Faustus" syndrome, we just might miss seeing the risen Jesus mysteriously present right there in the ordinary things of life, right there behind the ordinary faces that fill our daily existence. In the people and the chances that make up our regular routine, Jesus has already come and is already present. We don't need to hang on, waiting for some Faustus. The crucified and risen Jesus already speaks to us and acts for us right now. He does so through the things, occasions, and persons we know very well.

Can we afford to let our lives slip away, waiting for some Faustus? Can we afford to postpone living, as we dream about someone or something that will turn up one day, explain it all *to* us and fix everything up *for* us?

In a wonderful passage, St. Paul insists: "*Now* is the acceptable time; *now* is the day of salvation" (2 Cor 6:2). There is no need to wait for anyone else. Jesus is already among us. We can't afford to miss him. To do that would be to let slip away the acceptable time and to miss out on the day of salvation in which we already find ourselves.

For a short period of time, St. Augustine suffered from the "waiting-for-Faustus" syndrome. However, Augustine also had a hungry, restless heart. His deep hunger and restlessness eventually brought him into the presence of Jesus. There, his hunger was satisfied and he found a peace that no one could ever take from him. He never again gave into any "waiting-for-Faustus" syndrome.

Part Four

God

Part Four

God

1

Who Is God?

St. Gregory the Great used a marvelous image to express the rich depth of the scriptures and their meaning. The texts of the Bible, he said, are like "waters in which lambs can play and elephants can swim." One text that beautifully exemplifies this richness of the scriptures and their different levels of meaning is Exodus 3:14a when YHWH reveals the divine name: "I AM WHO I AM." This is a central verse for anyone who wishes to reflect on who God is and what God is doing for us.

Great theologians in the Middle Ages showed themselves to be elephants rather than lambs in the way they understood and interpreted this verse. For them God was revealed as pure being, as the God who is boundless, absolutely unconditioned, and totally necessary. God simply *is*—from eternity to eternity.

Many scholars came to reject that interpretation, which seemed to be a long way from the original meaning of the Hebrew text. But recently some scholars have tended to return toward that interpretation: YHWH is pure being, unlimited being, the God who is I AM. As YHWH tells Moses: "You shall say to the Israelites, 'I AM has sent me to you'" (Exod 3:14b).

YHWH, as other scholars noted, can also mean "He who causes to be." The name then does not indicate the eternal being of God but the divine presence and action in the events of history. Our God is the God who causes things to exist and causes events to happen. In all the things that come to pass and in all the events that are caused to be, YHWH is powerfully present. He cared for Moses and his people. Through Moses, YHWH then emerges as the God who cares for *us* in history and causes things to happen for *us*. This is another way of appreciating the drift of that mysterious divine name revealed to Moses.

"I will be what I will be" is a further possible rendering of what God discloses to Moses. In the 1960s, some theologians seized on that meaning to talk of YHWH as the God who, in a special way, is the God of the future. Our God is an "Ad-vent" God, the God who comes to us *from* the future.

These theologians connected what was revealed to Moses with a theme of the Book of Revelation: "'I am the Alpha and the Omega,' says the Lord God, who is, who was, and who is to come" (Rev 1:8). God is not described here as we might expect, as the One "who is, who was, and who will be"—that is to say, as equally related to the past, present, and future. By replacing the verb *to be* with the verb *to come* ("who is to come"), the biblical text highlights the *coming* God, the God of the *future*.

"Locating" God in the future means respecting the divine initiative, an initiative that goes beyond anything we can plan and manipulate. By acknowledging the futurity of our "Ad-vent" God, we acknowledge the divine freedom and creativity that elude and transcend all human control.

These then are three ways in which we can swim like elephants or play like lambs when interpreting the revelation of the divine identity to Moses. Our God is, first, a God with infinite fullness of being; second, our God causes and has caused things to be for us; third, our God is an "Ad-vent" God, who comes to us out the future.

Like Moses and the Israelites, we, too, have a God who spans our present, our past, and our future. Whether we feel like elephants or lambs, we can "immerse" ourselves in YHWH, our

God who here and now is the richest fullness of everything, who has caused things to happen for us in our history, and who will be our God in the future that comes to us.

━ ━·━·━·━·━·━·━·━·━ ━

2

What Is God Like?

Some years ago when I was still teaching in Rome, an up-and-coming painter came to town and asked if she might put a question to my students: What is God like? Being an artist, the young woman wanted the students to reply not in words but with some kind of painting or sketch.

She received back from the students all kinds of pictorial answers. That's what also happens if you ask people to reply in *words* to the same question: What is God like? They will give you a broad variety of answers to the question; their replies will complement each other and help to fill out the total picture.

One answer was put into a classical form almost a century ago by a German thinker, Rudolf Otto, and still enjoys some popularity. He called God "the frightening and fascinating Mystery (*Mysterium tremendum et fascinans*)." That answer pulls together the story of when Moses met God at the burning bush (Exod 3:1–6).

Moses was fascinated by what he caught sight of: a flame of fire out of a bush. The bush was blazing with fire, but not consumed. He turned aside to look more closely at this fasci- nating sight. But then he found the scene awesome and became frightened. He removed his sandals and hid his face. He was afraid to gaze at this manifestation of God. Moses experienced the presence of God as frightening, even terrifying. To cap it all, God revealed himself in a very mysterious way—with a name that is not a name: "I AM WHO I AM."

One can use Rudolf Otto's language to sum up the numinous episode. God encountered Moses as the frightening and fascinating Mystery.

The Jesuit order, to which I belong, was founded by St. Ignatius Loyola, a courtier and soldier who became one the most significant Spanish mystics of the sixteenth century. After he converted and founded the Jesuits, Ignatius received all kinds of wonderful graces and was blessed with a wide range of mystical insights that included some glimpses into the life of the Trinity.

Interestingly, for Ignatius *the* supreme gift he received was a profoundly loving reverence for God. For this saint and mystic, that was the grace of all graces: his loving reverence for God or reverential love for God. To be sure, he experienced God as the supremely *fascinating* Mystery, the mysterious God to whom he could give his whole heart. But Ignatius also experienced God as the *frightening* Mystery, the mysterious God who called for the deepest reverence.

Ignatius's reverential love for the mysterious God, or—as we might also say—loving reverence in the face of the divine Mystery, recalled something of what Moses experienced in the encounter at the burning bush. Ignatius's reverential love for God also anticipated the notion of God as "the frightening and fascinating" Mystery that was crafted in the twentieth century by Rudolf Otto.

A helpful way to think about this is our experience of *beauty*, which is also a fascinating and almost frightening mystery. I am sure that my readers have all been touched in various ways and at various times of their lives by the experience of human and divine beauty. It goes without saying that beauty is always fascinating. We are drawn to people and things that are lovely. We want to linger in the presence of beauty. But there is also a mysterious, even awesome, depth to those people and things that are beautiful. Where does their beauty come from? Why does it delight and captivate us? Why is it also somehow frightening, even terrifying?

Many centuries ago St. Augustine called God "the beauty of all things beautiful." God is wonderfully attractive and yet also awesome and even frightening.

We do well when we pray to be renewed in our sense of the mysterious God, the One who is not only sublimely awesome but also sublimely beautiful. "What is God like?" We can rightly answer out of our experience: "Awesome, to be sure, but also fascinatingly beautiful."

3

The God We Love

There is a glowing passage in the *Confessions* of St. Augustine that raises the central question: What is it that we love when we love God? Augustine replies in terms of our five senses: what we see, hear, smell, taste, and touch. There are many things that we experience physically through seeing, hearing, smelling, tasting, and touching them. That is not what happens when we experience God. And yet there is a kind of spiritual seeing, hearing, smelling, tasting, and touching involved in experiencing and loving God. Here is my translation of what Augustine wrote when addressing God in his *Confessions* (10.6).

> What is it that I love when I love you? Not the beauty of a body nor the glory of time; not the brilliance of light so pleasing to the eyes; nor the sweet melodies of all kinds of songs; not the fragrance of flowers, ointments, and perfumes; not manna and honey; nor limbs that welcome the embrace of the flesh. I do not love these, when I love my God.
>
> And yet I love a kind of light, a kind of voice, a kind of fragrance, a kind of food, and a kind of embrace when I love my God, who is light, voice, fragrance, food, and the embrace of my inner person.
>
> There shines into my soul that which no place can hold; there shines forth that which time cannot take away; and there is a fragrance that no breeze can disperse, a taste that eating does not diminish, and a clinging together that never loses its satisfaction. It is this that I love when I love my God.

In this passage, Augustine evokes wonderfully the created things that fill our senses. They are things that are too wonderful to be despised and yet our experience of them can never satisfy us fully and forever.

It is only the light, the voice, the fragrance, the taste, and the embrace of God that fill our hearts in a complete and lasting way. Augustine knew well the verse of Psalm 34:8: "Taste and see that the Lord is sweet." He knew, too, that it is only the experience of the divine sweetness that can fill our spiritual senses now and forever.

Let us quietly open ourselves and be ready to see, hear, smell, taste, and touch our loving and beloved God.

4

"...with all your heart"

Jesus said: "You shall love the Lord your God with all your heart....You shall love your neighbor as yourself" (Mark 12:30–31). Yes, but what does love of God and neighbor mean? What's the first thing we might say about love, the greatest commandment?

Love, to begin with, means approving of people, valuing them deeply, praising them, and rejoicing that they belong to our world. That's where we can start thinking about love and putting love into practice: by approving, valuing, praising, and rejoicing in other people.

Clearly, love is missing when we treat others in ways that are debasing and depersonalizing. A cartoon that appeared in the late 1960s showed a long-haired student passionately embracing a girl in bed and asking: "Why speak of love at a time like this?" Does sexual activity ring true and make any sense when it excludes the love that truly values "the other"?

It's obvious that loving God involves approving of God, being glad that God is there in our world. From the Jewish faith we have received that loveliest and shortest of prayers: "Alleluia." *Allelu-ya* means "praise YA," a shorter name for "YAHWEH." Yes, praise God and praise God for everything. Alleluia is a wonderful way of saying that we rejoice in God and love God.

Perhaps the more difficult challenge here is praising and approving of other human beings. But Jesus calls us to that. Loving those around us entails, at least, approving of them, being glad that they exist, valuing them all very deeply, and praising them from time to time.

When I talk about love, I often remember great writers like Dante Alighieri. He spent a lifetime trying to fathom the sublime reality of divine and human love. There was and is so much to say about love. You could fill the shelves of a library with the books that have been written about love.

But love means at least this: God approves of each of us. God rejoices that we are here and values us infinitely. Through Jesus, God invites us to do the same. With all our heart, we should rejoice in God. That love expressed to God should lead us to be very, very glad about all other human beings around us.

We often say Alleluia when we pray to God. We can and should also cry out Alleluia about all our brothers and sisters. Let's praise, value, and love them too, as we praise, value, and love our God.

_____

5

All Is Grace

Perhaps the most important and difficult lesson to be learned in our lives is this: Everything and everyone belong to God. We are in God's hands and they are good hands. God always acts with infinite wisdom and overflowing goodness. Our lives can seem filled with painful, and even cruel, failure. In some ways and at some levels, that may be true.

But, when set in the final balance, our lives are a sheer gift from God.

No modern writer has expressed this better than George Bernanos in *The Diary of a Country Priest*. That novel returns over and over again to the questions: How do we understand the lives we live in the presence of God? What is it all about?

The central figure in the novel is a young French priest who entrusts to his diary his experiences in a country parish. One day he writes: "My parish is bored stiff, no other word for it. We can see them being eaten up with boredom, and we can't do anything about it. Someday perhaps we shall catch it ourselves—become aware of the cancerous growth within us. You can keep going a long time with that in you."

With transparent honesty, the young priest describes the hopes he entertains and the disappointments he meets in his work for the parishioners. He burns himself out, and eventually will die of stomach cancer.

Along the way, he has a dramatic conversation with the local countess. She lost her only son when he was eighteen months old, she hates her daughter, and her husband has proved unfaithful. Her sufferings have made her bitter. When the countess confesses her bitterness and hatred, the young priest says to her: "God is not be bargained with. We must give ourselves up to God unconditionally."

But why should the countess or anyone else follow that advice? The answer comes through powerfully right at the end of *The Diary of a Country Priest*. It is because God has graced us and blessed us with everything which matters that we owe God everything in return. The whole of our existence is a free gift coming from God.

The novel closes when the young priest, already desperately ill from cancer, goes to visit an old schoolfriend who persuades him to stop overnight. Next morning, the host discovers the priest vomiting great quantities of blood. The friend describes what followed:

> The hemorrhage subsided. While I was waiting for the doctor, my friend regained consciousness. Yet he did not speak. Great beads of perspiration were rolling over his brow and cheeks. His eyes, which I could scarcely see under his heavy, half-closed lids, told of great pain. I felt his pulse, and it was rapidly growing weak. A young neighbor went to fetch our parish priest. The priest was still on the way. I felt bound to express to my unfortunate comrade my deep regret that such delay threatened to deprive him of the final consolations of the Church.
>
> He did not seem to hear me. But a few minutes later, he put his hand over mine, and his eyes entreated me to draw closer to him. He then uttered these words almost in my ear. And I am quite sure that I have recorded them accurately, for his voice, although halting, was strangely distinct. "What does it matter? All is grace." I think he died just then.

Through his novel, Bernanos articulates brilliantly the message: All is a gift from God. At the end, we never have a right to complain or grumble that we are treated badly. God does with us what he wills. And what God wills is always for our total and lasting good.

6

Our Hunger for the Trinity

The very first chapter of this book—"The Hungers of the
Heart"—spelled out something that I know in advance
whenever I meet people for the first time. All of them are
searching for three things. Every moment of their existence they
are yearning to be truly alive, to find meaning, and to love and
be loved.

First, we all want to live life to the fullest extent, to be
people who are truly alive. It's no wonder then that so much
publicity uses the theme of life and images of life. Recently I
spotted two advertisements that exploited this theme: one for a
cell phone and another for a TV sports channel. The cell phone
ad urged us to "live beyond frontiers." The sports ad encouraged
its viewers to "live the legend." Those who produce such ads
know the deep hunger for life that is within all of us.

Second, we all want to find meaning. We can put up with
much pain and suffering, provided it all makes sense. We find
our existence very hard if everything seems absurd and without
meaning. I remember a TV soap opera from a few years ago.
After we had watched a family being hit with some storms, the
central personality, an attractive wife and mother in her late
thirties, looked off into the distance and asked: "What's it all
about?" Her woman friend seemed equally puzzled about the
meaning of life and replied: "You tell me." We are hungry for
things to make sense. Where goals are clear and meaning comes

through brightly, we can cope with great, even immense, difficulties.

Third, we all hunger to love and to be loved. Love does make our world go round. We yearn to give our hearts to others and to be recognized and encouraged by those who love us.

We may describe the hungers of our human heart in various ways. Ultimately those hungers seem to take a triple shape: primordial desires for life, meaning, and love. We crave for a life that is utterly full and will never end; we search for a meaning that will throw light on everything; we hunger for a perfect love that will be totally satisfying.

It is the God who is Father, Son, and Holy Spirit who ultimately fulfills all that yearning and satisfies all that hunger. This is why faith in the Trinity is utterly relevant to every moment of our existence. Each moment of our existence we all hunger for life, meaning, and love; and it is in our tripersonal God that we find those hungers satisfied.

The Father, the first person of the Trinity, is from all eternity the source of all life, the One who has generated the Son and from whom proceeds the Holy Spirit. Within the existence of God and in the whole created universe, the God who is our Father and Mother, is the source of all life—life in utter, full abundance. As an early council of the Church put it, all life has come "from the womb of God."

The Son is the One whom we call the Light of the World, the ultimate Truth, the Teacher who shows us the way to move ahead in our existence. John's Gospel begins by calling him the Word: "In the beginning was the Word and the Word was with God, and the Word was God....And the Word became flesh and lived among us, full of grace and truth." We could rightly retranslate those verses by saying: "In the beginning was the Meaning and the Meaning was with God and the Meaning was God. And the Meaning became flesh and lived among us, full of grace and truth." Christ, the second person of the Trinity, is *the* meaning, *the* final truth, the One who gives light and meaning to our existence.

The third person of the Trinity, the Holy Spirit, is the mutual Love between Father and Son, that divine Love who is poured into our hearts. Many of us remember and sometimes still sing that popular hymn from the 1976 Eucharistic Congress: "You satisfy the hungry heart." The loving Spirit of God, the Holy Spirit, does satisfy our hungry hearts. At Pentecost, we regularly sing another hymn, "Come down, O love divine, seek thou this soul of mine." The Holy Spirit has come down. The Spirit of Love does seek our hearts and souls, and fills them with the glowing love of God.

Every waking moment of our existence, we are all yearning for the fullness of life, for a meaning that will light up our path through the world, and for a love that will satisfy our hunger and fill our hearts. It is in our God, who is Father, Son, and Holy Spirit, that we find the richly satisfying answer to our threefold search.

Hence, year by passing year at the feast of the Holy Trinity, I pray for the congregation with whom I am celebrating the Eucharist:

> *May you always find in our God*
> *life in all its fullness,*
> *the meaning that will show you what "it's all about,"*
> *and the love that will fill your hungry hearts.*
> *May the God who is life, meaning, and love*
> *be with you and stay with you always. Amen.*

7

Experiencing God in Prayer

"Who is God?" and "What is God like?" Perhaps the best short answer is "the One we experience in prayer." In a very real, if mysterious, way, praying consciously puts us into contact with God and lets us be touched by God.

The experience may seem quite obscure and difficult, like Jacob wrestling with God in the dark (Gen 32:23–31). But I have never known the experience of prayer to do anyone harm. Its results never fail to be good.

As with all experience, experiencing God in prayer is always a firsthand affair. It is something in which we *personally* engage, something that happens directly to us. No one can take our place in prayer. It is one of those things we must do for ourselves. People can give us innumerable details about some fabulous city, but they cannot literally take our place in personally visiting it. Likewise, no one can literally take our place in prayer, whether priests, saints, or anyone else.

In one of his few moments of humor, the great philosopher Immanuel Kant remarked: "No else can go into the water for us." Like swimming and learning to swim, we have to do it for ourselves. When we do plunge into the water and try to pick up some swimming style, we may prove very good at it and conform quickly to what some coach tells us to do. But inevitably, we will swim in our own way, moving our legs and arms around in our own individual fashion.

Without meaning to, Kant offered an image for our lives of prayer. When we plunge into prayer, we may learn to conform to some general pattern. But we all pray in our own particular way and let our specific experience of prayer happen within ourselves and for ourselves.

What does the personal experience of God in prayer look like? The psalms provide the classic answer. Those who prayed and composed the psalms bring us into the heart of prayer—with their cries of thanksgiving, joy, praise, loneliness, pain, and complaint. The psalms show us what the communion with God in prayer is like and invite us to let that kind of personal experience happen to us today.

The psalmists also let us glimpse every now and then that prayer can be difficult, even agonizingly difficult. It is no modern discovery that to pray and give oneself consistently to prayer can be hard and even heroic.

8

A "Countdown" Culture

We live in what has been called a "countdown" culture. We constantly find ourselves counting the days until something occurs. When that something occurs, we find ourselves counting the days until something else happens.

We may be counting the days until the weekend arrives and we can get away. Then we can catch ourselves calculating even the hours before we can head home. We find ourselves crossing off the days on the calendar in the run to Christmas. After the New Year, we check the dates of various birthday parties. We figure out how many weeks remain before high school closes down for the summer and we will have to work out what to do with our children on vacation. Or perhaps we count up the years that still remain before we retire.

There are so many deadlines to meet, schedules to observe, appointments to keep, and planes to catch. In our countdown culture we let our calendars, watches, and date books run our lives.

To be sure, this countdown culture has its positive side. Watches help us to be more productive and to maintain a wider web of relationships through the courtesy of being on time. But this way of existing can turn some things into a nuisance or at best into an unpleasant duty that we perform as fast as we can. Life will start again at five o'clock, when we have seen the last customer and can go home.

Even more alarming is the way the countdown culture makes us experience reality too much in relation to ourselves. There are X number of days before *I* must attend to such-and-such a job; there are X number of weeks before something else will call for *my* attention. Each of us then forms the midpoint of his or her own world and does so at a certain point on the time line. *I* have done such and such; *I* am preparing *myself* to do something else next week. In a countdown culture, we are caught up in the tendency to pursue our own ends, to cultivate our own thoughts and hopes, and to stop ourselves from being broken open to the mystery of our all-loving God.

There is the ever-present risk of having time only for myself and my projects. Sheer busyness can leave us deaf to the good news and blind to the mystery of God. We must take time out for God, and that—surprisingly perhaps—will mean taking time out for our real selves.

Many centuries ago, St. Augustine prayed: "Lord, that I may know myself, that I may know Thee!" We might adapt this prayer and say: "Lord, how little do I know myself! How little do I know Thee! Lord, that I may take time out to know Thee. If I pause to know Thee, I will begin to know also my real self."

If, on regular basis, I say no to the countdown culture and take time out for God, I will also begin to understand myself a little better. Nothing can be more important than knowing what is happening to me spiritually and where I am going on my way home to God.

9

Loving You Always

Many years ago the great songwriter Irving Berlin composed this lyric: "I'll be loving you always." At the time, a friend said to him: "People don't love each other always. Why don't you call your new song 'I'll be loving you Thursday'?"

Well, thank God, Irving Berlin refused to change the title and his text, and gave us his moving song as "I'll be loving you always." In a sense, of course, his friend was right. Unfortunately, many people don't love each other always. They *want* to do so. They would like to be loving and faithful for a whole lifetime, come what may. Yet we are weak. Little by little our love can grow cold. We can become unfaithful and unloving to each other.

But with God, things are different. God is always loving and faithful, come what may. God's love never grows cold. Our loving God is totally faithful and utterly loving to each one of us.

That is the heart of the message that Jesus brought us, the message that Jesus himself embodied. Jesus' being with us was and is God's way of saying to us all: "I'll be loving you always." There are no limits to this divine love. It goes on and on and on, not just for many years and not just for our whole lifetime. God's love for each of us lasts forever.

You must have seen that advertisement in jewelry stores: "Diamonds are forever." When a young man gets engaged and buys a ring, he wants the love he feels for his fiancée to last forever. He cherishes her deeply and yearns to love her always.

Alas, the love we yearn and hope for, we don't always find in ourselves. But we do find it in God. With God, "diamonds are forever."

When Jesus came among us, God was saying to us: "I'll be loving you always, not for just a day, not for just a year. I'll be loving you always."

Thank you, Irving Berlin, for your song. I am glad that you did not change your text, but kept those words, "I'll be loving you always."

Epilogue

In the Old Testament, the Book of Numbers contains many treasures. One of those treasures is a very old blessing, apparently used at the conclusion of worship in the Jerusalem Temple. The blessing goes like this: "The Lord bless you and keep you; the Lord make his face to shine upon you, and be gracious to you. The Lord lift up his countenance upon you, and give you peace" (Num 6:24–26).

In and through Jesus Christ, God has uncovered the divine face for us and let that face shine upon us. The gracious face of God has come among us and brought us peace.

May the crucified and risen Jesus, through the power of the Holy Spirit, continue to bless us all and keep alive within us that peace and joy that no one should ever take from us.

Index of Names